# INTRODUCTION

Until recently, researchers believed that your brain was "fixed" after early adolescence. In other words, whatever you have is what you are left with forever. However, presently, we realize that your brain has astounding abilities to change its very structure. Your brain was assumed to be "hardwired" for a defined mode of operation. This turns out not to be real. your brain is not hardwired, by experience, it's "soft-wired."

For instance, take Michelle. I was acquainted with her in Norman Doidge's superb book, "The Brain that Changes Itself." Michelle is in her 30s.

Like many of us, she cherishes great discussions, watching films, and reading. Although Michelle has a couple of incapacities and disabilities, she has a job, and from multiple points of view, her life is fairly customary.

What isn't normal about Michelle is that she only has half a brain. She's missing the whole left hemisphere because it never developed when she was in the womb.

It was recently imagined that various areas of the brain were given various functions, and if some portion of the brain were damaged, the corresponding function would be forever lost. Not really! Not only can the brain develop new cells, but it can also, like Michelle's right hemisphere rewire itself to assume control over the functions that her left hemisphere would ordinarily control.

The implications are significant. But what does that mean to you? If your thoughts and actions can change the physical structure of your brain, which thus impacts how you think and feel, that means you have significantly more power over your psychological and emotional states than was ever thought possible.

For instance, each time you stress or imagine something to be as awful as it can be, it's as if you simply hit an inner frenzy button, and your body will set itself up for flight or fight.

Have you ever noticed that when you think of that gathering you are scared of on Monday morning, or that call you continue putting off, or the troublesome customer or manager that you need to work with that your heart starts beating faster, your palms start perspiring, and your mouth goes dry like cotton? Adrenaline is flooding your system, and you feel disturbed simply thinking about it.

Each time you focus or stress on negative outcomes, you add another layer of worry to your system. Before long, you may not perceive how a lot of pressure and stress you are carrying, and unchecked programmed reactions will continue pushing through your body. Various researches have recognized that specific physical reactions to negative feelings and uncertain pressure can drain us of energy. No big surprise we often feel so tired!

In an ideal world, you would understand that thinking about something that has not happened is a false alarm. When your brain would make an impression on your body, which would rapidly relax back to ordinary. However, with our bustling ways of life and the steady stream of commotions, interferences, and stressors (both imagined and real), our bodies have overlooked what it intends to truly relax.

To exacerbate the situation, what we presently think about the brain is that after some time, if you continue hitting the panic button, it will learn how to be stressed. Then it will begin hitting the panic button for you even when there is nothing to panic about.

But the inverse is also true. If your brain has learned how to be stressed, there are things you can do to rewire your brain so you can experience more happiness, energy, and fulfillment in life, even during challenging circumstances.

So remember, your astounding brain is incredibly affected by the day-to-day considerations that you have, and you can wire it for progress and joy or misery and failure - it's up to you.

# Chapter 1

# THE SCIENCE OF NEUROPLASTICITY

**Can your mind change your brain? The answer is absolutely yes!**

Learning how to do this, and draw in your neuroplasticity is the second step of my training program.

To start with, it is vital to recognize your belief structures. It took me a long time to perceive the intensity of this in my own life and exactly how much it was in control. Belief structures make up the undetectable filter through which we see and interpret the world, and every one of us has our very own unique structure that has been developed from the day we were born. It's our "truth about the world."

Note that it's our truth, and isn't a reality with regards to the world. We've made belief structures that served and upheld us at once. However, as we grow and advance, they become constraining and even damaging. The reason this is step number two is that you should initially get clear without anyone else belief structures before you can transform them. Moving them into cognizant awareness is the initial step to their change.

Beliefs can be exceptionally strong, however, they can also be constraining. It's the constraining ones we have to distinguish so we can start discharging them, and ourselves, into progressively far-reaching and satisfying experiences.

One of the most energizing parts of doing this work is that you are changing your physiology. Habits, beliefs, and old methods of perceiving the world are simply detectable thoughts made up in the mind; they are engraved patterns that exist in your physiology. This is good and bad. Good because once we learn something, it tends to remain with us - we don't need to think of how to tie our shoes, drive a car, brush our teeth, or any other things we do every single day. We have engraved our physiology to do these things naturally.

Although, the "awful" old belief that never for once serves us runs on automatic, as well! It's these old propensities, patterns, and beliefs we need to change and grow. These are simply the parts that are presently keeping us away from the success, love, freedom, happiness, and power we desire.

Science is currently discovering "How the Brain Rewires Itself." A phenomenal article by that title ran in "Time Magazine" on January 19, 2007, outlining and featuring the most significant studies in this field. Incredibly, these studies uncovered that "mental preparing can change the physical structure of the brain." And these aren't quack researchers performing this work. These studies are being done by neuroscientists at driving institutions like Harvard Medical School, the University of California San Diego, the University of California Los Angeles, the University of Toronto, and the University of Wisconsin at Madison.

These studies reveal how "The brain can change because of the thoughts we think... something as pathetic as an idea can influence the brain, adjusting neuronal associations in a way that can treat psychological instability, or maybe lead to a more prominent limit with regards to compassion and empathy. It might even dial up the supposed happiness set point." The specialists are calling this newly found function of the brain "neuroplasticity."

Why is all this so significant? Since this new information discloses to us that by practicing desired, feelings, thoughts, and actions, we can rewire ourselves to experience (and make) the world as we want.

Identifying your belief structures and learning how to deliberately develop your thoughts, also your experience is a key part of my coaching system.

<u>Try this:</u>

Watch your thoughts cautiously. Pick a day to intentionally watch and track your thoughts via bringing a little journal with you as the day progresses. On different occasions throughout the day – maybe every hour or so - record the "nature" of your thoughts. Have they been mostly positive and imaginative, negative and ruinous, or increasingly neutral? Celebrate and strengthen the positive innovative thoughts you are having, and question the more negative and ruinous thoughts. Ask yourself "are they true?" There is a possibility that the negative thoughts are not true. Keep in mind, life is dynamic, and what was once valid, may never again be!

Thus, you can start to extricate the grasp of the more negative idea patterns and open up to increasingly innovative reasoning, positive experiences, and great magic!

## THE NEUROPLASTICITY REVOLUTION

- **How to Optimize Your Brain Every Single Day**

Recent brain studies show the long-lasting ability of the brain to rewire itself, responding to what we think, feel, and do every single day. You may then wonder, "If that is true, what lifestyle can help me improve my brain?"

Brain fitness is our brain's ability to promptly make extra connections among neurons, and even to advance new neurons in specific parts of the brain, also to maintain significant functions, for example, memory and attention.

- **What Recent Brain Research Says**

Recent logical research shows that a particular lifestyle and activities can improve the wellbeing and level of the functions of our brains. Such improvement can occur because of neuroplasticity, then the rate of creation and endurance of new neurons in specific parts of the brain is increased. Alternately when the rate of creation and endurance of synapses (the connection between neurons) accelerates, or when a neurochemical environment is persistent in our brains to help data processing.

The good thing about finding out that our lifestyle that can influence brain capacities is that it puts our brain health generally under our control. However, there is no magic recipe. Researchers are just starting to see how, and what we do can connect with our genetic makeup. There will never be an explanation of every one of the difficulties inherent in maintaining one's brain health. Most neuroscientists believe that a huge number of approaches will be important.

## BRAIN FITNESS AND ALZHEIMER DISEASE

Brain fitness may assume a role in deferring the development of Alzheimer's-related side effects. A lot of research has been led on healthy aging in the last two decades. Various components have been related to the diminished dangers of building up Alzheimer's disease. Among these variables, mental exercises run very high.

People who remain mentally active and occupied with side interests all through their lives reduce their danger of building up Alzheimer's disease and other dementias. In a recent report directed by Dr. Yaakov Stern, driving analyst on the cognitive reserve, people with the most significant level of recreation exercises exhibited 38% less risk (controlling for other factors) of building up Alzheimer's side effects. For each extra sort of action, the risks were diminished by eight percent.

It is believed that mentally stimulating leisure activities or exercises assist in building up a cognitive reserve. This can help to delay the appearance of dementia's symptoms. Interestingly, education also appears to have a protective impact. Researchers have discovered that knowledgeable individuals are less exposed to age-related brain fitness decrease. Significant levels of training have also been related to lower risk levels for Alzheimer's disease. As indicated by Dr. Arthur Kramer, the two key lifestyle habits that may help somebody with deferring Alzheimer's symptoms and improve general brain health are to remain physically active and to maintain deep-rooted intellectual commitment.


**The 4 Pillars of Brain Fitness**

So what factors affect brain health?

Recent rules establish good nutrition, managing pressure well, mental exercise, and aerobics. Other factors may also have an impact. Dr. Elizabeth Zelinski frequently calls attention to that "it is also imperative to maintain emotional connections. Not just with ourselves, to have self-esteem and self-confidence, but also to our friends and family." Sleep and overall health conditions are different factors that also matter.

In summary, there are four key brain fitness pillars to consider:

- **Balanced nutrition:** Generally, what is useful for the body is also useful for the brain. Eating an assortment of foods of various colors including cold-water fish that contains omega-3 unsaturated fats and avoiding highly processed foods with added ingredients are suggested. Vegetables, especially green, leafy ones, are also recommended, whereas few well-known supplements have shown long haul benefits on memory and other subjective capacities.

- **Stress management:** Chronic pressure or stress lessens and can even repress neurogenesis. Meditation, yoga, and other calming exercises are viable in countering pressure. Biofeedback gadgets that measure heart-rate changeability and show feelings of anxiety constantly offer more high-tech options to manage stress and pressure.

- **Physical exercise:** Physical exercise has been shown to upgrade brain physiology in creatures and people. Physical exercise improves learning through the expanded blood supply and the development of hormone levels in the body. Of all the types of physical exercise, cardiovascular exercise that gets the heart beating - from strolling to skiing, tennis, and b-ball - has been shown to have the best impact.

- **Mental stimulation:** it reinforces the neurotransmitters or connections between neurons, subsequently improving neuron survival and subjective functioning. High-quality brain exercises involve novelty, variety, and challenge.

Please note that these pillars are integral, they don't substitute one another. It is significant for every one of us to perceive our beginning stage, and recognize what pillar we need to concentrate more on. For every pillar or lifestyle factor, it is essential to be innovative in finding a routine or schedule that works for a person through error and trial. As per Dr. Workmanship Kramer, the perfect way is to join mental and physical stimulation alongside social association: "Why not go for a decent stroll with friends to talk about a book? We all lead very busy lives, so the more fascinating and integrated our exercises are, the more likely we will participate in them."

## IMPROVE YOUR BRAIN'S NEUROPLASTICITY THROUGH GENTLE MOVEMENT EXERCISES

On a scale of 1-10, how much do you love your body and appreciate what it accomplishes for you?

If your answer isn't positive, you're not the only one. However, you're also constraining your ability to accomplish ideal health and achievement. I unequivocally urge you to develop a positive relationship with your body since it will change the trajectory of your life!

Your brain and body are occupied with a constant discussion, each impacting the function of the other. Many people know about "mind over matter," the idea that we can utilize our will to control or train our body. You may have heard of professional athletes who envision an excellent exhibition before they enter a challenge. However, most people don't understand that their "matter" also influences their brains. That is why it is basic for well-being to tend to your body. Concentrating on improving your coordination and simplicity of movement, what I call self-use, will help your body feel extraordinary and improve the structure and capacity of your brain.

Individuals who meditate frequently, focus on their breathing, however, there are numerous parts of your movement that you can extraordinarily improve through attention. When you start noticing the components of how you move, you'll gain another understanding and significant appreciation for your body. Focusing on sensory cues will also rewire your neural hardware to make you progressively organized and light on your feet, lessen or take out incessant agony, and make more opportunities for positive thoughts to flash through your consciousness constantly.

One proven approach to simultaneously organize your body and improve your brain was made by Dr. Moshe Feldenkrais (1904-1984), an Israeli physicist and judo master. Dr. Feldenkrais' advanced neural movement utilizing novel "exercises" which comprise of delicate movement with consideration. The way toward adapting better movement propensities turns into the impetus for stimulating neurons in the brain to make new connections.

When you comprehend the standards of Dr. Feldenkrais' strategy, you can apply them to improve any movement-related feature of your life: sitting easily, running, piano playing, golfing, or even vision! So how does it work? His technique uses human living being's intrinsic procedure of figuring out how to improve functionality. Throughout our lives, the brain changes in size and capacity as it makes neural associations in light of sensations perceived by the body. This procedure is called neuroplasticity. Dr. Feldenkrais found that movement could be significantly improved by offering a sensory contribution to little units that the brain could consolidate into patterns of neural connections. He comprehended that human potential is the procedure of the brain growing perpetually unpredictable and refined limits. He called attention to the fact that intelligence and maturation are less a matter of age, but rely upon the level of brain function that an individual accomplishes. Also, there is no restriction on how far we can improve our brains once we realize how to do it!

Dr. Feldenkrais also found that as an individual's ability for efficient, effective movement expanded, their reasoning turned out to be more positive and imaginative, less "stuck." There is a relationship between building up our brain's sensitivity to notice insights regarding our movement and a growing subjective ability to process information. The more details we can see, the higher our awareness, and the more alternatives we have to settle on decisions about our behaviors and thoughts. As movement improves, the mind becomes less "reactionary" but rather more "response-able." As we supplant movement propensities, for example, poor stance or breathing, which are neurologically connected to pressure and tension, we gain courage and free ourselves to work from the most significant levels of human awareness and decision.

For decades, people have utilized Dr. Feldenkrais' exercises to perform better and to resolve physical issues such as balance, repetitive stress injuries, back pain, and simultaneously experience advantages, for example, emotional and cognitive limitations, relief from anxiety, and back pain. When you experience improved functioning through this simple brain-body feedback, you can't resist the urge to increase a critical appreciation for your body's role in your growing feelings of wellbeing and strengthening. It's the loyal partner who's been with all of you all along!

# HOW YOU CAN OUTSMART YOUR BRAIN WITH NEURO-SCIENCE

The first time I read that my brain was plastic; I thought it was a joke. That was until I understood the author wasn't talking about plastic as in a plate, however, as in pliable.

As brain imaging innovation has progressed, so too has our comprehension of how the brain functions. One of the most critical discoveries has been the disclosure that our brain doesn't stop developing when our body does, that it can adjust and change straight up to the end of life. This means that we have entrenched methods for handling information and reacting to our environment, we are still fit for developing new and progressively helpful procedures later on. While a more profound comprehension of neuro-plasticity is incredibly significant for individuals who have suffered from a stroke or other traumatic brain damage, what has provoked my curiosity most is its application for those of us whose brains work impeccably well.

Neuro-plasticity research now proves that you are never too old to even consider changing and that you can rewire your brain to think in manners that lead to more prominent success and happiness. I should concede, however, my illuminated comprehension about my brain's "plasticity" has been both a benefit and problem. Never again would I be able to justify my inability to figure out how to back-up my computer with excuses like "I'm simply not a technology individual." However, though at times, I've reviled my freshly discovered information about my brain's capacity to ace abilities that have since evaded me, develop healthy habits, and adapt better approaches for reacting to natural triggers, eventually this information has been incredibly significant. I presently realize that the adage "You can't teach an old dog new tricks" is only a bogus and helpful conviction that spares us from the exertion involved in adapting new tricks - like backing up my computer.

I attended a coaching meeting where Dr. Jeffry Schwartz, UCLA Professor of Psychiatry and creator of "You Are Not Your Brain," talked about his exploration discoveries on neuro-plasticity. What he shared strengthened my understanding and affirmed what I naturally knew and expounded on in my book. Which is, that by purposefully choosing to view your environment in new ways, revise your own story, and step into action in the presence of your fears, you become more capable in whatever those activities maybe, but also construct your "courage muscle" so you can react more viably in various aspects of your life. Whether in the discussions you have with your work associates, your confidence in affirming limits in your own life, or your eagerness to take on objectives that you've recently avoided, by practicing better approaches for interacting in your environment, you can assemble new pathways in your brain and produce new (and better) results in your life.

Neuro-scientific discoveries, similar to those also detailed in Dr. Norman Doidge's earth-shattering book "The Brain that Changes Itself," have shown that right to the end of our lives, we can fabricate new neural pathways in our brain that eventually rewire it. It takes repetition, or building up another habit that usurps an undesirable old one, or even another method for managing individuals and life - regardless of whether it is timidity, pessimism, or laziness - it takes practice. Repeated practice. It took your whole life to build up the default ways of thinking and acting that you have today. Rewiring how you think and act is going to take time.

Self-coordinated neuro-plasticity may sound all very intellectual and high-brow. However, at its core, it's pretty simple: building mindfulness - the structure hinders achievement in each field of life. That is, developing your capacity to watch yourself with the goal that you observe, as a disconnected observer, what you are feeling and thinking, and how each is feeding off one another at any given moment. This is essential since you can settle on new and more valuable decisions when you are aware of the ones you are making now. Just like a one-time walk off the beaten path will not create a new pathway on the forest floor, neither will a one-time activity make another pathway in the brain. Rewiring how you think and act requires redundancy and time.

## The S.O.A.R2 Approach to Outsmart Your Brain

As you've been reading this, you may have thought of certain aspects of your life where you aren't feeling as positive or powerful as you might want. I welcome you to practice self-coordinated neuro-plasticity and rewire your brain's default method for reacting by working through every one of the following five stages. They contain my S.O.A.R2 Model for conduct change and strength fabricating (the fundamental structure hinders for "SOARing" higher than ever of achievement in work, love, and life!)

1. **STOP** what you are doing and observe your thoughts and how they are making you feel. If you are feeling extremely anxious or uptight, take at least five deep breaths to cut off the base brain's "Alarm" response and avoid what is generally called a "neural highjack."

2. **OBSERVE** the way you look at your circumstance. What is it about how you are looking at this "issue" that makes you feel the way you do? Imagine yourself up high, noticeable all around, looking down on your circumstance and notice how by raising your viewpoint, it can change how you see the "issue" and with it, growing the options for settling it.

3. **ASK** yourself how the smartest individual you know sees your conditions? What's the significant exercise this circumstance needs to teach you? (Furthermore, trust me, each awkward feeling and troublesome circumstance has something of extraordinary value to show us.) Remember, we prove we are brilliant by our answers but insightful by our inquiries. The more you can grasp interest, the wiser you will become.

4. **REFRAME** your circumstance, remembering that the considerations you are believing are not reality, exactly how your brain is processing it. How, by surveying this from a bigger point of view, may you be able to see the "issue" in a different light? Concentrate on what you can do, not on what you can't.

5. **RESPOND** deliberately to your circumstance (especially from simply responding the way you may have always done previously). What is the most valuable approach to react to this circumstance?

## NEUROPLASTICITY IS HOW TO CHANGE YOUR BRAIN TO BE HAPPY, HEALTHY, AND SMART

"Each man can, if he so wants, become the sculptor of his brain." Santiago Ramon Y Cajal.

After completing a lot of research, present-day neuroscience has at last reached the unavoidable resolution that we can stop affliction, heal diseases, and improve our prosperity by training our brains and psyche to think unexpectedly. This is possible as a result of a brain procedure called neuroplasticity.

Neuroplasticity is the life-long ability of the brain to change and rewire itself. Neuroplasticity occurs because of various stimulations: learning, new feelings, life experiences, and emotions.

### Why is this possible?

It is possible because new neurons (brain cells) keep on developing all through our lives, even at a very old age. Besides, neurons continually make new connections between themselves because of new beneficial experience. It looks like this: New Experiences = New neurons + New Connections between Neurons.

### Can the brain changes be estimated and seen?

Indeed, these brain changes can be physically estimated and seen on brain scanners like MRI, PET, EEG, MEG, and others. Presently we can see the consequence of psychotherapy (counseling, brain exercise, and such) utilizing brain checking systems.

### What kind of condition and sickness can be helped with Neuroplasticity?

Most conditions where the brain is included (mental, spiritual, emotional, and even physical) can show signs of improvement with appropriate brain training. These are OCD, eating disorders, fears, depression, strokes, anxiety, brain, trauma, obsessions, addictions, and much more.

### Are there any negative effects of neuroplasticity?

The ability of the brain to change itself is surely uplifting news. It makes the brain more powerful and resourceful than initially thought. However, it also makes the brain more vulnerable to outside impacts producing more negative and rigid behaviors.

Many of our bad conditions and habits are the consequence of the brain's versatility. Anything that includes unvaried redundancy - our culture, careers, home environment, personal habits, even personal thoughts, and feelings can lead to rigid behaviors.

For instance, repetitive negative emotions about yourself and your body can prompt eating disorders. Prolonged personal disappointment with the environment, home, and close individuals can lead to fixations and various types of addictions. Many demanding occupations which include an excessive amount of reasoning and planning can create unfortunate propensities of over justifying everything and losing the association with our instinct and the emotions in our hearts. Some cultures produce inflexible practices in people dependent on cultural and religious perspectives. Every one of our neuroses is the result of neuroplasticity.

**How to utilize neuroplasticity to get the best results?**

It is important to understand the substance of your brain: to recognize what are the rigid negative practices you have to change, or what positive propensities you need to create. The second important step is to pull together on a positive, healthy, preferably pleasure-giving conduct (activity) which will supplant the negative conduct.

When you work with neuroplasticity, it isn't what you feel while you are practicing neuro-plastic activities; it is what you do that matters? The fundamental battle isn't to surrender to the feelings.

With neuroplasticity, the more you do it, the more you need to do it, and the less you do it, the less you need to do it, which will have a significant effect on the result.

A powerful urge to change your brain is required or at least some kind of motivation to change.

**Can all people's brains be changed with neuroplasticity?**

Everybody's brain can be changed to a specific level. The limit points of changing one's brain are totally and unpredictable reliant upon ones want to change, the exertion put into the evolving procedure, the strong condition, and the general wellbeing of the individual can have any kind of effect.

The extent of damage to the brain from past awful programming also assumes a role. However, don't surrender; it is also notable that some gravely damaged brains recuperate well and now and again far better than the brains with lesser harm.

# Chapter 2

# REWIRE YOUR BRAIN, BODY, AND SOUL WITH SUBLIMINAL MESSAGES

Few people utilize subliminal messaging to get what they need through their words. Subliminal messages can have a compelling effect on the human brain. Subliminal messages have a direct effect on the intuitive brain with no acknowledgment. In previous decades a few promoters have utilized this strategy to boost deals and sales and the outcomes were additionally incredible.

In this way, subliminal messages assume a fundamental role in overhauling the psyche of people. Some people don't accomplish their objectives because of the obstructions of their thoughts in their sub cognizant personalities. Subliminal messages or one can say, hypnosis is a procedure by which the masters remove these blockages from their minds. This is a treatment that is utilized by a few analysts while treating their patients.

Subliminal procedures are also utilized for self-awareness and it is much the same as brain programming. The therapist goes into the oblivious brain and clear the psychological blockages. These blockages are the primary reasons, responsible for the downgrading of one's life. One can say these blockages are negative considerations or negative forces.

Subliminal strategies can help individuals in evacuating these negative thoughts or blockages from the brain. There are chakras in the human body that are liable for human wellbeing, riches, and other things. The negative forces or considerations enter the human body or mind when the chakras are not in their proper position. In this way, subliminal messages are extremely useful in realigning the chakras of the body to get the best in life.

After the expulsion of negative thoughts from the body or mind, they are supplanted naturally with positive forces. Bit by bit, they start making positive thoughts and help in modifying the self-confidence.

However, subliminal recommendations don't work overnight or promptly, but this strategy helps those individuals who truly need to change their way of life and need to accomplish their objectives in life. Thus, subliminal messages are the most ideal path for revamping the brain, body, and soul adequately.

# HOW SUBLIMINAL AUDIO REWIRES YOUR BRAIN

It is very possible to rewire the brain, body, and soul by utilizing the subliminal messaging technique. There are different ways through which one can rewire one's brain. One of the most significant techniques for reworking is subliminal audios.

However, there are some specialists, therapists, or doctors who utilize this strategy to improve the intensity of the brain. Therapists can utilize a communication path for the treatment of patients, however, this is likewise one of the powerful approaches to treat the patient. Subliminal messages are utilized viably in the development of a kid's brain and empower them to study with concentration and core interest.

The subliminal audios are utilized in different ways like for improving memory control and for self-confidence or self-help. One can get these CDs from any of the nearby bookshops, and if they don't have, then one can request the same order.

Subliminal audios are for self-confidence and stunning memory as well as being utilized in immense variety and some other needs that incorporate subliminal audios, for example, to get in shape, quit smoking, get motivated, passing an exam, and many other needs.

Subliminal audios are becoming a genuine method to control one's mind and other changes that influence the character of the individual. Subliminal messages are positive assertions and imperceptible statements which are centered directly at the sub cognizant mind.

The inaudible statement work like repetitive thoughts that enter the brain, overwrite all the negative thoughts and supplant them totally with positive considerations and a positive attitude. The entire procedure works for the individual who truly wants to improve.

Subliminal audios are the ideal approach to get associated with the inward thought and to upgrade the learning potential. One can work or build up the psyche proficiently.

# Chapter 3

# TRAIN YOUR BRAIN, IMPROVE YOUR LIFE

It occurs instantly and it is over before you even notice. Three seconds is all you need to establish an incredible first impression when you meet people for the first time. It is all the time it takes for the other individual to frame an idea regarding you, based on your looks, your habits, your clothes, and your body language.

Every time you meet another person, the very same procedure takes place. Unfortunately, you never have another opportunity to establish a good first impression. These first experiences practically set the pace for all the following relationships. This is the reason they are enormously significant, particularly if the individual you're meeting influences your profession or your public activity. That is why you ought to constantly remember the significance of making a good first impression.

When you read all the guidance that therapists and professional advocates give out concerning making an incredible first impression, you understand that a lot of the things they say are identified with a frame of mind and great habits and little is said about looks. However, somehow people rather improve their looks first.

The reason behind such a decision isn't clear, however, it mostly includes a profoundly established conviction that it is practically difficult to change yourself. It's taken you all your life to become what your identity is, and that what you are is a comprehensive thing, encompassing the good, the bad, and the ugly. Also, individuals give a valiant effort to change outwardly, trusting that it will likewise affect their inside. Young ladies get a makeover and guys exercise on steroids.

What they don't understand is that even if they may get a shock of adrenaline from those outer changes, it may be a temporal one. In the long run, the novelty will blur away, and they will return to being their previous selves.

Some will most likely begin the cycle all over again.

It doesn't have to be that way. You have the power inside yourself to change and turn into a better individual than you are presently. You should simply give more attention to your brain. Truly, that very same organ that you have ignored for such a long time, which by the way is liable for everything that goes on with your body. Your brain can rewire itself, to reconstruct all your constraining convictions and your deepest fears so that you can begin working at full steam. Neurologists call this brain plasticity.

Brain plasticity is at its highest when you are a baby. From that point on, it gradually fades but never vanishes. If you utilize your muscle, if you exercise it regularly, it becomes more grounded. However, if you don't exercise your muscle at all, it debilitates and inevitably decays. The same occurs with your brain and its plasticity.

Research has shown that our brain produces electrical impulses when our neurons communicate with one another, which happens constantly. These driving forces are called brainwaves and range in recurrence, relying upon the sort of activity that you are performing. Interestingly enough, neurologists have found out that external stimuli can have an impact on brainwaves, to the point that it is possible to actuate the brain into explicit perspectives. Along these lines, if you want to double your ability to learn or build your profitability, brainwave training can give you a hand.

A lot of brainwave training items have been created in recent years. Of those, BrainEv, short for Brain Evolution System, is absolutely the best. It joins three distinctive brainwave training strategies to deliver quick, quantifiable outcomes. And you should simply listen to a sound CD for 30 minutes per day, six days per week, for half a year. You will start getting results soon enough. Your memory and your imagination will build, your dozing/sleeping pattern will improve, you will be in complete control of your life.

As you can see, it is very possible to change. It has always been. Customarily, meditation was the chosen way, however, it took long periods of training before you'd begin to see any result. BrainEv doesn't take that long and you can get results right away. Consider BrainEv a workout routine for your brain. It will make you feel extraordinary about yourself and will also help you look great.

Have you ever tried and tried to break a habit just to surrender in two weeks, believing you will just always be unable to change? Habits, even potentially great ones, are difficult to break for a reason; neurons that fire together wire together. This implies that your brain structures neural pathways by discharging chemicals that stimulate delight and motivational circuits. With reiteration, a habit is framed cutting out highways in your brain.

The habits we structure, regardless of whether bad or good, address our issues, relieve stress and nervousness and give adjustments. When we get the result, we're motivated to repeat the conduct that is provided.

For instance, after dinner you and your life partner watch a favorite TV show (cue), you sit together on the couch and unwind (routine) and have one of your preferred chocolate bars (reward). You've currently made a feedback loop: when you consider sitting in front of the TV, you consider relaxation and chocolate!

This may not be an issue except if you're overweight, have severe diabetes, or wouldn't fret about being addicted to chocolate. However, what if you have a seemingly good habits which is like being a perfectionist?

That was the situation for my customer Suzanne. She was a single working mother who was worried and depleted. She was inclined to making a few subjective contortions (thinking blunders) every day, one of which was white and black thinking.

Suzanne went through childhood in a home where the family their idea was to "always be the best." If she didn't' do everything impeccably, she felt like a disappointment. This caused her enormous tension. If she failed, she would beat herself and panic (routine conduct) then she would take a pill to calm herself down (reward). The issue was the anxiety relief her reward provided was short-lived. Whenever she felt "short of anything," she returned to popping pills like chicklets.

To support her, I showed her the "art of taking note." I asked her to start paying attention to her negative self-talk, her real signs that revealed to her she was beginning to encounter uneasiness, and what she believed about herself. I also instructed her to see the reasoning errors she was making and gave her some unwinding strategies to calm herself.

By uplifting her mindfulness, Suzanne learned how to get a grip on her uneasiness before it overpowered her. Rather than reacting to her anxiety cues how she had, she interfered with the feedback loop by testing her contemplations with positive counterstatements and profound breathing. This provided an enduring compensation of serenity.

Because Suzanne would not like to pass on her anxious propensities and her perfectionist ways onto her children, she was excessively motivated to change.

Breaking habits requires purposeful, intentional practice to change the neural systems in our brain. The uplifting news is it very well may be done on account of the brain's neuroplasticity. Here are a few hints on the most proficient method to start the rewiring procedure:

**Practice self-awareness**

You can't change what you don't see, so start by focusing on what you're directing your attention to on a minute-by-minute premise. Listen to what you let yourself know. Is your self-talk, for the most part, negative and condemning?

**Practice gratitude**

For people who will generally observe the glass half empty, gratitude is an extraordinary propensity to develop. I advise my customers to record at least two things every day they can be grateful for. After some time, it starts to change your point of view astoundingly.

**Get Motivated**

Breaking habits does require solid motivation on the front end. You must have something that motivates you to change. In Suzanne's case, it was seeing her bad habits being reflected in her kids. In case you're tired of being sick, if you're tired of feeling hopeless about yourself, that may be sufficient. No one but you can choose, however, once you have, you should practice positive thinking to re-wire the neuro-networks in your brain.

**Practice being intentional**

In the past few decades, there has been a series of research about the neuroplasticity of the brain. That is an extravagant way of saying that the brain can rearrange itself by making new neural pathways to adjust, as it needs. When learning another task, making sense of an issue, or attempting to defeat an impediment, you need to focus. The more you practice and focus on something, the better you get at it (the new aptitude that you're trying to learn or the issue you're trying to settle). This activity of concentrated practice and redundancy shapes new neural connections in the brain as synapses that don't usually fire together, presently do.

Brain science has given us so much new and energizing information. Change isn't just possible, it's profoundly likely if we follow a portion of the previously mentioned rules. If you're tired of replaying all the negative tapes in your mind, and tired of being stuck in the regular old dysfunctional patterns, try some of these procedures for at least six weeks and see what occurs!

## YOUR BRAIN, PHYSICAL EXERCISE

Every activity you take part in, thinking, includes your brain. Your brain, physical qualities of it, and how we use it to learn are all topics that have recently been explored. The aftereffects of this research have been applied by Posit Science and this has prompted Brain Fitness to be all the more at that point created. Indeed, Brain Fitness and its co-founder, Dr. Merzenich are receiving consideration and inclusion for giving individuals more when the brain works out. He's given a technique, a treatment, and plan to numerous individuals who look for brain exercises to balance, slow, or stop indications of ailment or reactions of chemotherapy or drugs. It is a sad reality, but the number of inhabitants in individuals meeting this standard is developing quickly. Fortunately, the specialists and discipline of cognitive science are working faster. The outcomes are already being applied.

Your brain will benefit and change for the better if given the correct input. There is a similar hypothesis with muscles, isn't that so? You work your legs out with specific exercises, such as running, and you get results. The same is true with the brain, physical exercise, with a program like Brain Fitness, brings about expanded intellectual and brain ability. If you exercise your brain, you can get results in as little as a couple of days. This is because the brain has astonishing abilities and one is to rewire itself as new information repeatedly comes in; the right input and exercise are the key, not the unnecessarily different programs. Think smart and avoid the commotion online; view the research and instruct yourself further. In the case of searching for yourself, you'll be happy you did and if this is for somebody you know or love, at that point everybody around you will likewise benefit from your commitment and time to figure out a way to help.

# Chapter 4

# YOUR BRAIN – USE IT OR LOSE IT

Generally, when I consider aging well and living a better life as I grow older, I consider the state of my brain. Our brains are ravenous beasts that can develop disabilities without enough mental movement, physical action, and appropriate nutrition. In this way, if keeping your brain sharp and active is essential to you, here's some guidance in every one of the territories.

**Mental Activity:**

Even in old age, the brain can develop new neurons. Putting extreme mental decline caused by infection aside, most age-related loss in memory or motor skills result from inactivity and an absence of mental exercise and stimulation. Research also shows that the brain becomes more grounded and sharper as long as you keep on utilizing it. For instance, avoid reading into your brilliant years, keep on increasing the rate of speed that you read, and the measure of information that you can read. All our abilities show signs of improvement with time if we keep on utilizing them, including knowledge and problem-solving skills.

If you proceed to challenge and engage your brain with exercises such as continued learning, expanding your points of view every day and taking part in activities that require you to think, react quickly, evaluate information rapidly and precisely, and proceeding to extend your brain muscles, your brain will remunerate you with expanding great memory and intellectual skills.

Basic things, similar to even more formal education, can contribute to the intellectual stimulation of the brain and may even reinforce the brain cell systems to help in preventing mental function damage. Having a decent feeling of self and realizing that the things that you do in life have any kind of effect and accepting that you are adding to the benefit of everyone has appeared to diminish the psychological decrease in older adults.

**Physical Activity:**

Physical activity positively affects the brain and brain functioning. Low-effect activities such as strolling or swimming are particularly great since they increase blood flow which builds the oxygen and glucose that arrive at your brain which is especially beneficial to the brain's proper functioning.

Low effect activities that are not strenuous prevent your muscles from taking up additional oxygen and glucose, so you can adequately oxygenate your brain. Development and exercise increase breathing and pulse with the goal that more blood flows to the brain, improving vitality creation and waste removal. Studies of senior residents who walk routinely indicated significant improvement in memory abilities contrasted with inactive older people. Strolling/walking additionally improved their learning capacity, focus, and unique thinking.

**Proper Nutrition:**

The foods we eat influence how the brain functions: tone and vitality level and how it handles its assignments. Research in labs around the nation shows that proper nutrition can improve mental capacities and perhaps even avert physical brain aging. Here are five hints on food for the brain:

1. Balance your glucose/sugar to give fuel to your brain. Refined sugar is a part of the simple carbohydrates family which fuels the brain, but just for a brief timeframe. What we need to get are some complex carbohydrates. Fruits are an amazing source. Rather than a short explosion of energy, these starches have long chains of sugar atoms that the body separates step by step, discharging glucose to fuel the brain after some time. Mental exercises go through your glucose, so eating complex carbohydrates at each supper is an incredible method to keep brain energy paced all through the day. Berries and citruses are high in complex carbohydrates and antioxidants which diminish the danger of subjective debilitation.

2. Eat basic fats to guarantee brain wellbeing. The health of your brain depends not just on how much (or little) fat you eat, but on what kind it is. Mental execution requires the particular kind of fat discovered most commonly in fish, known as omega-3 unsaturated fats. Different types of fat can undermine knowledge.

3. Include a lot of protein-rich nourishment for your diet. Having

protein at every supper adjusts glucose levels and makes synapses which are vital for the reasoning procedure. Include lean meat, eggs, soy, cheese, or nuts to a snack or meal to restrain the retention of sugars/carbohydrates.

4. Eat foods that are rich in minerals, vitamins, and antioxidants to protect your brain. Studies prove that dietary intake of antioxidants from vegetables and fruits essentially diminish the danger of creating intellectual impedance. Vitamin E and Vitamin C and beta carotene repress the creation of free radicals.

5. Keep your brain very much hydrated. Given that your brain is around 80% water, the primary standard of brain nutrition is adequate water to hydrate your brain. Indeed, even slight dehydration out can raise stress hormones which can harm your brain after some time. Alongside your 80 ounces of water a day, juice, for example, grapefruit juice, has the same effects on the brain as vegetables and fruits alongside the hydration benefits. Green tea is also useful for brain function as it contains chemicals that upgrade mental alertness and relaxation.

The brain can adapt and rewire itself. Indeed, even in old age, it can develop new neurons. While infection can cause a serious mental decrease, most age-related loss in memory, mental capacities, or motor abilities originate from the absence of mental exercise, physical exercise, and proper nourishment. At the end of the day, deal with it, and it will stay nearby and take care of you.

## FEED YOUR BRAIN – KEEP YOUR MIND

For quite a while, we've been advancing the role of a healthy lifestyle in keeping up brain fitness. Another new study lends more help, but before we get into that, we thought we'd center around some common-sense topics regarding why this is valid.

One simple idea to comprehend that doesn't require a Ph.D. is the fact that any organ in your body, including your brain, needs a healthy blood supply to get access to oxygen and nutrients. This is one reason why mental health problems and heart disease, including dementia are so frequently related. If you tied a tourniquet around your leg to remove the blood supply, you shouldn't be astonished when your foot quits working too well.

The same goes for your brain. If you keep on doing things that are not good for your cardiovascular system like sitting around throughout the day and eating chips, your vascular system will have an issue, and this isn't good news for your brain. Your brain utilizes about 20% of the oxygen that you inhale and the calories that you eat. Your blood supply is dependable to get that substance to the ideal spot in order to keep your brain in great working operation.

The advantages of long-lasting learning and ceaselessly moving your mind to keep it sharp are settled. However, if you don't couple that exertion with doing what's important to keep up a healthy neurovascular system, you can't completely understand the benefit. You may have read a lot about neurogenesis and synaptogenesis, which is the constant rewiring of your brain that happens when you remain rationally dynamic and keeps your mind agile. However, this procedure can function admirably if the veins close to such an excess of rewiring are sufficiently healthy to carry out their responsibility. Where are the energy, oxygen, and nutrients essential for the redesigning work going to originate from?

Consider neurogenesis another housing subdivision going into a current community and the roads as the blood supply to service the houses. If you were the builder constructing this new development you wouldn't get anywhere if you didn't initially take care of the new roads. Not only are the roads required for the new proprietors to get in and out of their homes, they are also required for delivering all the wood and concrete, allowing the various groups to come in and build the new houses, and remove all the refuse. Also, new brain cells or new brain cell connections need healthy roads (neurovascular system) to work properly.

Related to this, an enormous study, simply divulged for the month (April 2008) by Dr. Thomas Montine from the University of Washington, reports that 33% of the danger of dementia originates from a sickness of little blood vessels in the brain. In this 12-year study, 3,400 people over age 65 volunteered for occasional intellectual testing and a brain autopsy upon their death. In the 221 autopsies performed, scientists found that small blood vessels accounted for around 1/3 of the risk for dementia. Significantly, this kind of small blood vessel ailment may go unnoticed for quite a while. We're not talking about huge problems like a stroke or blood clot obstructing a huge vessel. However, after some time, these little issues can add up, and bring about an intellectual impairment.

This study originates from the Pacific Northwest, the origin of grunge-rock, and Starbucks coffee. We can't be certain that every one of these individuals isn't experiencing some sort of post-apprehension psychological issue or a latent flannel shirt sensitivity! We also can't rule out suffering from some type of post-traumatic worry after attacking the world with expensive coffee, proportional to about $18.00 per gallon, somewhat more than we're currently paying for gas. One of us (Evans) was brought up in Seattle and might be showing some early symptomology.

Although, with these potential confounds aside (except if Austin Powers was correct, and during the time that Dr. Evil was cryogenically protected, his faithful cronies invested vigorously in Starbucks), this study is an unimaginably significant step that outlines the different factors that can lead to dementia. Much more significantly, it recommends that you can generously diminish your chances of creating dementia by attending to lifestyle factors that can ensure against vascular infection.

The magnificence is that we have an intelligent thought of how to do this since veins serve to supply active zones of the body with nutrients! So if your brain is active (which requires energy), and you're maintaining vascular wellbeing by eating right and working out, chances are that you will be enormously lessening your risk of developing dementia from little vessel disease. Presently, it ought to be noticed that research is ongoing regarding this, however, common sense would propose that this will remain constant.

Taken together, this features some significant reasons concerning why nutrition and exercise assume such a crucial role in brain fitness. Taking care of both of these lifestyle factors is important to maintain a healthy blood supply and the production of fresh blood vessels, to nourish new brain circuits built up by learning and mental activity. If you disregard this part of brain fitness, you may restrain your ability to profit from neurogenesis and synaptogenesis instigated by numerous individuals of the 'brain-training' programs intended to keep your mind young.

At this point, it's gotten clear to most that practicing yoga goes a long way pass having long, lean limbs and impeccable posture. It is turning out to be all the more evident that yoga is a lifestyle. This lifestyle starts in the studio, however, it has a ground-breaking method for penetrating all aspects of your existence by hacking into your brain and changing how you manage different circumstances. Thus, yoga becomes not what we do, but how we do it.

Yoga is the act of syncing breath with movement, remaining calm while doing a challenging activity. This is the reason for the sensational change that happens in our brains when we practice. While we practice, we re-adjust the way we experience emotions such as loneliness, anxiety, and stress by taking advantage of the systems that make those feelings and changing the grooves in our brains.

Regardless of what the circumstance may be, whether it's running from a tiger or taking a final exam, the nervous system has one reaction to stress. This includes muscle tenseless, negative thoughts, shortness of breath, and the release of cortisol into the circulatory system. At the point when we stay shaped and control our breath while placing our body into uncomfortable positions, such as doing a headstand or bending into a revolved bound half-moon, the brain gets reconstructed to react proactively and to stay loose in an unpleasant circumstance.

This activity hacks the brain by setting off specific feelings and afterward rewiring our regular reactions. Taken far enough, this empowers us to take advantage of the high potential functioning of our being to achieve whatever objective we put forward.

When we learn how to lessen self-judgment and fear through yoga, the potential outcomes of life open up and everything we desire gets charged towards us. The act of falling all over, attempting to do flying pigeon, or lifting your leg one inch higher in the third warrior tells your brain that your doubts don't control you. By going towards discomfort and uncertainty in our poses, we register that our fear of what will happen just exist as restrictions, and naturally have no validity or power.

By practicing yoga we not just shape our bodies, we shape our brains and saddle the incredible power we hold inside. Go forth in confidence towards your practice, and realize that each struggle is in the highest interest of your body, brain, and soul.

# Chapter 5

# THE UNIVERSE INSIDE YOUR BRAIN

This chapter has been named after a part in the incredible personal development and business development book called "The Answer" by John Assaraf and Murray Smith. This book has had such a constructive effect on my business and individual life that I felt constrained to share what I have realized and how I have applied it in my existence.

John Assaraf has been studying personal growth philosophies as well as brain science for 25 years. When he alludes to a "universe" within our brains, he makes a fantastic analogy. When I think about the universe, I think about an enormous cluster of systems and procedures that stream together in perfect harmony. And that is actually what our brains do. With the most developments in science and technology, we currently find out about the brain than at some other time in human history.

Because of that, anybody keen on making progress or achieving success, building up their potential and living a satisfying life would be exceptionally wise to spend some significant time finding out about this "supercomputer" we have in our heads. Whether you understand it or not, your brain has been customized to control your behavior and is legitimately liable for the outcomes you are creating in your life. This is where "The Answer" comes in and where I have been able to actualize some extraordinary thoughts.

One lesson that had a critical effect on me was the way that our cognizant brain is responsible for just two to four percent of our behavior. This implies that 96-98% of what we do every day is managed and controlled by our nonconscious brain. We don't need to consider these tasks, they are taken care of without our cognizant awareness. Examples I have seen for myself include sitting on a seat, getting dressed, writing notes, chewing food, and even driving my vehicle. These tasks required my cognizant consideration sooner or later prior in my life, however, through reiteration, have become "installed" in my nonconscious brain.

What's amazing is that it is practically difficult to list out all the activities we perform every day because there are such huge numbers. With the awareness that only two to four of these activities require us to think, it turns out to be very evident that utilizing will power or other comparable forcing capacities to arrive at a significant objective in life is purposeless. The real solution is to reinvent the nonconscious section of the brain with the goal that those programmed activities work for us and push us toward our objectives.

Here is an instance of how I have made this work. Knowing that I had many goals that I had not yet reached and being aware of this conscious/nonconscious relationship, I was able to sit down and mentally review my self-limiting thoughts and behaviors. Some of my models include sitting around, reading emails that aren't important, reacting with outrage when a situation didn't go as planned, eating a snack when I was not genuinely hungry, beginning a decent business book, but not finishing or actualizing it (the list goes on too). By just becoming mindful of these nonconscious propensities, I have been able to sort out my very own improvement schedules to supplant these activities with progressively positive empowering ones.

Another lesson that I learned from "The Answer" has to do with what a few people call 'self-image' or on account of this book, the 'thermostat in your brain.' This thought was initially portrayed in the 1950s by Dr. Maxwell Maltz in his famous book "Psycho-Cybernetics." This part of our brain is responsible for keeping us free and safe from danger. It additionally keeps us on track with a set point, much like a thermostat would accomplish for the temperature in a house or an autopilot would do for a plane. The issue is that our self-image defines the boundaries of our usual range of familiarity, thus, it can keep individuals from making a move that will bring them joy and achievement if those actions require perceived risk.

For me actually, I have constantly had the objective of having a shaped figure with low body fat and decent muscle mass. While I have been quite disciplined at keeping up a wellness schedule, my thermostat was not set at a similar level as my objective. I had always been somewhere in the range of 20-40lbs overweight for most of my life. Eating and drinking propensities were my greatest challenge points.

When I originally got settled in self-improvement, I began to roll out some physical improvements. I got down extremely near my optimal bodyweight after years of trying to do as such (I had done so once in the past just to restore all of the weight). Although I endeavored to get to that level regardless, I didn't have the particular body shape and tone that I had always longed for. Despite my endeavors, despite everything, I had waiting propensities for (eating and drinking), in hindsight, I didn't understand was problematic until I began studying the ideas in "The Answer."

When I found out about the way toward 'rewiring your brain' to make critical and lasting changes in personal outcomes, beneficial things started to occur. Generally, if we need to instill another propensity into our behavior, we need to "physically forge new neural pathways within the tissues of your brain." This isn't a procedure that occurs overnight, but instead, something that requires significant time and repetition.

When I comprehended this procedure and studies of what was going on within my brain, I recognized what I needed to do to arrive at my fitness objectives. I made a multi-day challenge for myself. The challenge incorporated the demonstration of three significant behavioral changes:

1. A type of physical exercise each day for ninety days.
2. Healthy eating regimen and ceasing from eating pass feeling full for ninety days.
3. Refrain from every alcohol drink for ninety days.

I have likewise made some visual reminders of my optimal body that I have put all over my office so I see them consistently.

By the end of this initial ninety-day test, I will have a new system of accomplishment that I can use for the rest of my life to ceaselessly expand and grow my capacities and improve my every day propensities with the goal that they bolster the objectives and dreams I hold for my life!

# Chapter 6

# REWIRING YOUR BRAIN – THE BASICS

## How Your Past Programs Your Brain

There aren't many of us who can say we've left our childhood unscathed or have had fantasy relationships. We've all had some downright awful things transpire. Some are worse than others. Time after time, we playback those negative memories again and again until they're a piece of our whole mental makeup. All that you do is guided by how you see your past.

Believe it not to be true? If you're continually battling with weight, cash, as well as love... this is an unmistakable sign that your past is in the driver's seat!

Want more proof? Think about a fantasy you have. This could be returning to school, escaping from Mr./Ms. Wrong, or at long last leaving that dead-end job. What happens when you imagine this? Things spring up everywhere to prevent you from pushing ahead. You can't get past the manner of thinking, not to mention putting in the effort to make a better life.

Maybe you feel confused, afraid, stressed, unworthy, or even anxious. You come up with a lot of reasons not to seek happiness. That is your past controlling you. That is all of the negative, screwed up individuals you came across throughout your life who contributed to programming your brain.

## Exercise: Reprogramming Your Subconscious

Right here, at this moment, refuse to harp on your negative considerations any more. All it serves is to cut your energy level down and encompass you with an emanation that keeps anything good from coming into your life.

1. When a negative idea about the past comes up rationally, shout "stop!"

2. In some cases, I'll sing a song as noisy as I can either in my mind or out loud. Your objective here is to deliberately assume responsibility

for your thoughts.

3. When you've interrupted this thought pattern, replace it with a positive memory that is comparably amazing. For example, say you were abused as a kid and a specific occasion flies into your psyche. Rather than yielding to the memory, raise a happy memory you have and review it in, however, as much detail as possible.

4. If you do not have very many happy memories or think that it's difficult to come up with something when pain or anger strikes, make a list of some more joyful occasions when you're feeling great and read this list when you're feeling down. Until I showed signs of improvement at rerouting my thoughts, I would read my list five times each day or more.

5. You could even write down future occasions you plan to experience. If you were in an awful relationship, record what you require in your next relationship. (Be sensible, however, because no one's perfect!) Write down what your future mate will look like and some happy occasions you'd prefer to impart to him/her. This is also an extraordinary method to program your psyche and energy field into drawing in what you want most.

The past is gone, it's done and over. The only way it can have any impact on you presently is if you let it. Those "terrible memory" pathways have worn a groove in your mind, so it's a lot simpler to review them, in any case. Decide to reconstruct your thoughts and see the difference it makes in your state of mind, and your life.

Have you noticed that positive experience appears to be more fleeting than negative experience? You may have a remarkable excursion or give the most splendid discourse and get rave reviews, however, the following day you find that your mood has emptied. Then again, when you make an error in broad daylight or have a misunderstanding with a customer, you likely stress about it for much longer than that.

This natural brain predisposition towards focusing on the negative bodes well from a survival point of view. Those of our mammalian ancestors who were relaxed and centered around getting a charge out of the beneficial things in life were bound to get eaten by predators than the apprehensive ones who were continually looking for danger. Primates who recalled what was hazardous and trained their young to be anxious about the danger had more accomplishment in passing on their genes.

Fortunately, a basic practice will efficiently rewire your brain to supplant your negative bias with a positive bias. This practice was created by Rick Hanson, Ph.D., a neuropsychologist and Buddhist instructor, author of "Hardwiring Happiness," and co-author of "Buddha's Brain."

You may have heard the expression "Neurons that fire together wire together." What this implies is that neural pathways that are utilized often develop more grounded associations. Our positive and negative encounters over a lifetime shape our neural habits.

For instance, if you suffered trauma in your youth, almost certainly, you confronted foundation anxiety as part of your enthusiastic state growing up. Then again, if you ponder every day, all things considered, you experience a resilience field of stillness out of sight of your emotional state.

Rick Hanson's act of "Taking in the Good" brings your brain into a benchmark state of enjoying the abundance that is accessible to us. New disclosures like these are energizing since brain researchers have identified easy routes to make changes that used to take long stretches of coaching or therapy.

**Below are the steps of this practice:**

1. Set aside five minutes.
2. Choose something accessible to you right now that fulfills you. It may be the case that you are loved by individuals who are exceptional to you. It may be the case that you have an awesome meal planned for tonight, or that you are paid to do work you love. Whether you are injured or sick, you can concentrate on the amicable working of each other piece of your physical body.
3. Focus your consideration on receiving this positive experience consistently for at least twenty seconds.

That is it! It's that simple. In case you're just like many of us, your mind will meander and oppose focusing completely on a positive encounter. However, what this 20 seconds does is to give the brain sufficient opportunity to move the experience of enjoying what's great from short-term memory to long-term memory, and along these lines gaining from it.

## HOW TO GET RICH REWIRING YOUR BRAIN

Wealth starts from within; you need to get rich inside before you get rich outside. This is one thing many people don't get, and that is the reason you know about individuals who win the lottery and end up broke in barely months. You also have poor at heart individuals who hit it big, however, end up broke following two or three years, or even months. Indeed, they had a ton of cash, however, despite everything, they had a poor mentality, so once the cash was all gone, they didn't know how to get it back. Henry Ford, the mid-twentieth-century American industrialist was once asked what he would do if he lost all his fortune, and he said he would restore everything within a brief timeframe because he would never be robbed of his genuine riches, which lies in his brain.

That is what you ought to comprehend before you continue reading this book; genuine wealth is in the brain, and that is the place that ought to be mined, and not outside. Many individuals have been raised with the mindset that it is difficult to get rich, or that you can't get rich if you were not brought into the world with a silver spoon, or that wealth is a terrible thing; these aren't accurate thoughts, and they prevent you from getting rich. You have rationally subjugated yourself from wealth if you have any of these perspectives; your job ought to be tied in with rewiring your brain to think otherwise, to get rich. I guarantee that once you start thinking like the rich, it would just involve time before your very own wealth finds you.

The main thing to know is that you are the co-maker of your life, that means you pick your very own fate. I have discovered that many people, particularly from the part of Africa believe that God has already written out their lives, and there is nothing they can do to transform it. You have to change your idea if you additionally think along these lines since it is false. In all actuality, God has given every individual the free will" to pick whatever he or she wants to be in life. That is the reason it is said in the Bible that "as a man thinketh in his heart, so is he." So, what you truly have business with is changing the way you think.

You become what you believe, you believe what you think, and you think what you see, hear, and talk. The last sentence merits reading a second time, and a third time, as that is where your answer lies. Since you realize you have the ability to get rich by rewiring your brain, what you must be keen on is the way you will accomplish that. Also, the most ideal approach to do that is to change what you feed your brain, rationally that is. Along these lines, feed your mind through your most responsive faculties; read books and articles that talks about securing wealth as not a hard undertaking; listen to motivational course accounts that discusses how you can get rich from nothing, and visit beautiful places while having it at the top of the priority list that you afford all that.

While you do this, you start having another point of view to life, and you should also back it up by having affirmations that you state for all to hear each day. You could state affirmations like-"cash flows to me easily." As it is stated, your words are an imaginative force and get to your brain, which is the innovative industrial facility. Furthermore, analysts have additionally found that words said reliably, regardless of whether false, are over the time accepted to be valid by the individual saying them. Also, when you think something, it will turn into a reality in your life. For whatever length of time that you follow these means, you will begin changing your inner-self, building it to perceive wealth as its regular state, and once you can accomplish this, once the internal and the external are the same, nothing would be difficult to accomplish, including getting rich.

For over 100 years, "The Science of Getting Rich" has been accessible to direct us to wealth in our lives, yet how many of us have acknowledged it and genuinely applied the information and intelligence it contains? How many of us have learned how to get things done in the "specific way" that prompts achievement, or how many of us even comprehend what the specific way is? Oftentimes, we are captivated by the title of the book and we give it a snappy read through, offer a little empty talk to it and the following week it is overlooked alongside its lessons.

The book is put on a rack or the footstool and is before long gathering dust alongside our plans to excel and gain wealth for ourselves and our families. How can we change this? How can we make the exercises it contains so convincing that they connect and snatch us and carry us along to success?

One approach to do this is to enroll the intensity of hypnosis to study the book and rewire our brains. We read the book and haul out thoughts and fold them into hypnotic suggestions to install in our subliminal. At that point, the thoughts will work normally in our lives as they stream out of us.

Hypnosis is simply the way toward giving recommendations while in a relaxed or a modified state of awareness. The alpha, theta, and delta states are viewed as relaxed hypnotic states and can be prompted by giving yourself recommendations to relax while slowing your breathing to a profound and customary rate. It can also be valuable to listen to music with a similar beat rate. Largo music like the classic "The Four Seasons" is a case of music that will help moderate the body and instigate this modified state. There are additionally numerous recordings available today that will help induce relaxation, utilizing these while offering relaxation proposals will be valuable.

After slowing your reasoning and your breathing and entering the adjusted state, you can start offering explicit proposals dependent on "The Science of Getting Rich." These recommendations will be extremely powerful when given in this perspective and they will slip into your subliminal, waiting to be activated by conditions where they will be useful. You will become adapted to live "The Science of Getting Rich." You will wake up anticipating the beneficial things that are in the world for you. You will start to draw in everything that you need in your life as your mind starts working with you to accomplish them as it is rewired.

# REWIRE YOUR BRAIN TO OVERCOME INSOMNIA

Why do we trouble with insomnia? An excessive number of us consider NOT going to sleep, rather than pondering, getting the chance to sleep when we hit the pillow at night. Frightful thoughts about not being able to rest, trigger the fight-or-flight reaction and the stress chemicals subsequently make us anxious, and keep us from relaxing.

As we become more prone to stress, we can't get the opportunity to rest, we manufacture a solid neural I-can't-get-to-sleep pattern in our brain. This pattern naturally relates to the fear of not being able to lay down with the very act of heading to sleep every night. Voila! The insomniac is born!

Many give little consideration to coordinating their thoughts. Many people believe that you need to think about whatever idea springs up in your brain, in any case. Nothing could be further from the truth. Efficient individuals have constantly realized that they can pick what thoughts they wish to think, and they can decline to think the dissident, self-defeating, keep-you-conscious thoughts that come running unbidden over their mind.

Fundamentally, if we don't know how we think, we won't know why we have a sleeping disorder. People should know the essential neuroscience of how they get from one idea to the next. This type of information is significant. When you know how your brain functions you can make it work for you rather than against you.

If you haven't considered why you think the thoughts you do, you likely don't the know the distinction between contemplating going to sleep and thinking about not going to sleep. It took me some time to comprehend the distinction myself and I'm a therapist. When your eyes are opened to it (no joke intended) you can see that the difference is simple but enormous.

If the prevailing idea in your mind is that you can't get to sleep, it will be hard to do so because the brain constantly reads the bearing of its most present predominant idea. Resting is a specific neural pattern that the brain normally reads, but not if frightful considerations become predominant over your common getting the chance to-rest neural pattern. Then you trigger the battle or flight reaction and stress chemicals flood the brain which makes sleep as inconceivable as 10 cups of healthy coffee before bed.

When you exercise a muscle, you make it healthy. When you exercise an idea, you make it prevailing. You exercise an idea by considering it and over again repetitively.

The act of getting to sleep is to intentionally, as an act of will, pick neutral, quiet, exhausting thoughts repetitively and make them predominant, supplanting the prevailing frightful idea that you can't get the chance to rest. After some time you can re-wire your brain out of its insomniac pattern.

You can manufacture another neural pattern that naturally triggers when you get into bed. You can construct a neural bridge, with neutral thoughts and mind exercise, that connects you consequently to the normal neural pattern of falling asleep.

My expertise is to help individuals re-wire their brains to escape depression. However, I saw that these same methods that attempted to re-wire your brain to escape depression also worked for insomnia. As individuals age, they wake up more regularly around evening time and these activities can help them, as well, to return to sleep.

Here are certain instances of mind exercises for insomnia. The first is designated "Make the Problem the Solution." Suppose you are trying to get to sleep and a faucet is dripping, or there is clamor outside, or someone's wheezing. You can use the irritating commotion as a meditation or mantra to help you get to sleep.

Simply close your eyes and relax your body. Then say to yourself, "With each sound of the dripping faucet, I am going deeper and deeper asleep." Hear the sound, and repeat the reflection. Picture yourself feeling the sensation of falling each time you hear the sound. Falling deeper and more profound. The reiteration of this exercise can frame a neural pattern to connect the words "deeper and more profound" to the hard-wired neural procedure of falling asleep.

Another exercise is to trick the brain into trusting you are sleeping regardless of whether you aren't sleeping. Simply continue saying again and again to yourself, "I am asleep, I am sleeping. Whatever thoughts I believe are simply dreams, since I am asleep. Whatever sounds I hear are dreams, since I am sleeping. I am sleeping. I am sleeping."

Something very similar occurs with this exercise. You re-wire your brain out of its fearful can't-get-to-sleep neural pattern by making a neural bridge from your prevailing idea "I am sleeping" to the brain's natural going to sleep neural pattern. The more you practice the exercise, the more grounded it turns into the neural pattern.

"The Clever Accountant is another exercise." Emotionally, we must be clever accountants. We should never, for example, carry the disappointments of today forward into tomorrow.

As we are getting ready for bed, it is extremely simple to slide into the regrets if we have over-eaten. It's easy to beat ourselves up if we have taken some horrible social belly flop, haven't completed the report, or didn't get the house cleaned.

However precise these thoughts might be, it is just not accommodating to our brain at all to think them, particularly when we are trying to get to sleep. We shouldn't take these thoughts to bed with us any more than we would take our vacuum cleaner or our golf clubs. These things are helpful, much the same as thoughts are valuable. But, they are not suitable for sleep time.

Thoughts of  disappointment or failure, for example, places our brain in contact with an unending number of negative neural connections in our mind (via learned affiliation) that will trigger the fight-or-flight reaction that prompts pressure. Rather, we should continue carrying forward our victories, however small.

If we can't amplify some achievement in our mind, we should continue repeating the little things as a sort of positive-train of reasoning which can "thought-jam" those unshakable negative contemplations into silence. Yes, perhaps we didn't get in shape today, however, we shed two pounds so far this month. Yes, perhaps we over-ate but there was most likely some little thing we left behind.

"Hey! I didn't eat that third brownie. I was triumphant over the third brownie. Also, in any case, it didn't taste great. Perhaps I'm becoming wary of junk food. I'm losing my desire for junk food. I believe I'm beginning to need to eat better, to eat healthier." It's even a triumph of sorts to state, "Hello, I did over-eat, and now it's over. It's gone. I am liberated from what I did today forever because today is before long proceeded to thank heavens for that."

Our little triumphs don't need to bode well when it's all said and done or even in the less stupendous plan of our lives. They simply have to be certain so they will interface with other positive thoughts in our mind by learned affiliation. This is a mind trick like some bookkeeping is an accounting trick that becomes mathematical, not necessarily common sense.

The significant procedure, as opposed to the particular substance. If we have been truly low functioning, it is a triumph to have brushed our teeth or to have cleaned up. For those of us who are high functioning, maybe we didn't win the Pulitzer this year, however, we have done the main section of our next book.

Remember that our pain is the very same whether we are low functioning or high functioning. So the triumphs, however little, can bring us equivalent emotional relief. The intrinsic significance of triumphs isn't pertinent. The way toward being sure is a higher priority than the content of the positivity.

Brushing our teeth is no less positive than writing the main part of a book. It will have a similarly positive outcome, by learned association, with whatever positive mentalities exist in the neurons of our brain.

Not exclusively are we interfacing with the positivity in our brain rather than the negativity that can trigger the fight-or-flight reaction, but we are re-wiring another more grounded positive neuronal pathway out of stress and anxiety with every great idea we think. This is the pathway to the regular procedure of falling asleep: practicing tedious activities of calm acknowledgment.

Even nonsensical thoughts repetitively thought will replace stressful thinking. I wake up every two or three hours myself.

I wake up every two to three hours myself. Usually, to return to rest, I simply grab for the last two to three words of the sentence that I thought.

## THREE WAYS TO REWIRE YOUR BRAIN IN ONE DAY

By making three little changes in your habits and routines, you can make your life unique and closer to the way you need it. These modifications don't require you to change. Individuals hate change to the exclusion of everything else in life since they realize it takes energy, commitment, and resolution to make changes in their life. Presently, you can modify your life by rewiring your brain marginally, utilizing almost no effort.

This magic formula for rewiring was initially intended for top leaders in organizations and non-profit organizations. They guaranteed that they didn't have the opportunity to go through training classes, read books, or whatever else that would constrain them to change to turn out to be increasingly viable. Besides they would not like to do what worked for another person since they KNEW it would not work for them.

Constantly, you play out an assortment of basic habits or tasks without truly considering how you're doing them. These habits are simple since you don't need to consider them to complete them. Something as basic as brushing your teeth, preparing to get down to business (assuming you still have a job), watching TV, preparing a meal, or browsing your email just requires a modest quantity of thought on your part. If anything intrudes on the procedure, you rapidly alter and proceed to finish the assignment. It is in this capacity to alter and go on where you can have an immense effect in your life in a brief timeframe.

<u>Here are the three brain rewiring modifications:</u>

1. Most adults have all the time. Next time you shave, start on the opposite side of your body. Try not to use your other hand to shave, you could cut yourself gravely. Use your rule hand, as you normally do, and essentially start on the opposite side of your body. Men, this typically implies starting with the other side of your face than your normal starting position. Ladies, it usually means starting with the opposite leg or underarm. Be cautious, this is somewhat tricky from the start.

2. Now, a slightly harder alteration that is somewhat progressively compelling. Move your wristwatch to the opposite wrist. Most people discover this modification baffling, aggravating, hard to achieve for more than a short time. The result is that they are truly compelled to take a look at time distinctively and their brain in some cases revolts and they need to return to the 'old method for' taking a look at time. Anyway, the brain has been rewired and the change has happened because they have done some little undertaking differently.

3. Take an alternate course to work whether you're driving, walking, or using public transportation; use an alternate beginning time or a slightly different route. There are various ways for you to get to

work. Do you know every one of them? Taking an alternate course enables your brain to be active again during the time it takes you to get from home to work. If you are extremely bold, take an alternate course on your way home as well.

Now that you are done laughing at doing three easy things differently, here is the reason for doing them. If you are eager to accomplish something unexpectedly, your brain will start to see two things:

1. There truly is an alternate method to complete this assignment.

2. This new way may be easier than the 'old' way.

Now, you may be saying, "Making my life different can't be that simple." Okay, keep on doing what you've always done and you will keep on getting what you've always gotten. Do you need your life to be diverse in superb positive ways? If so, be eager to do three little things <u>DIFFERENTLY</u> for a couple of days until you see that, indeed, you can do things any other way. Also, if you don't care for the distinctions you can generally return to your old ways. Your brain will be rewired diversely by then, and you will be unable to return to a less productive way.

## HOW TO QUICKLY REWIRE YOUR BRAIN TO ACHIEVE MAXIMUM PROSPERITY

All manifestation starts in the mind. It doesn't matter what it is you are searching for or need to have in your life, to show it you need to start by realizing you have it in your brain. There are some extremely simple steps you can take to adequately rewire your brain to amplify your prosperity. If you can get familiar with these four simple ideas and apply them, you will have the success you want.

**T-F-A=R**

This is the simple equation that clarified the procedure of appearance. You have to realize this condition to guarantee that you have the achievement you are searching for and all the prosperity you desire. The "r" is results and your outcomes depend on your "a," action. This is where the vast majority stop, they think if they make a move they will get results. The problem is our results are brought about by "f," our feelings. Our feelings originate from somewhere and that is the explanation we have to deal with when rewiring your brain. Our emotions originate from the "t," our thoughts. If you can get your contemplations in agreement with your objectives, you will flourish.

### Be aware of your thoughts

The way to boosting your success is to deal with your thoughts viably. The most simple approach to do this is to simply slow down, yes that is it, slow down. Take two seconds between something occurring and responding to it. During these little moments of two seconds, be aware of what thoughts are coming into your mind. If you feel the thoughts are aligned with where you ultimately want to go then proceed. If the thoughts are not in agreement with your future goal, at that point figure out how to change the idea so it is in greater alignment. When you can deliberately change your thoughts to be in an agreement with your objectives, you will see an expansion in your prosperity.

### Know precisely what you want in your life

Here is the key to having the option to put your thoughts in alignment with your ultimate objectives, you must be clear what those ultimate goals are. Know exactly what success means to you in as explicit of details as you can. The more explicit and clear you are in your ultimate objectives, the more powerful you will be in showing them. When you have clarity, it makes it a lot easier to adjust your thoughts viably. This is how you rewire your brain to build your prosperity.

### Know it before you see it

The last key step to rewiring your brain is to ensure the entirety of your thoughts agree with you realizing you have what you want before you see it. This is the last phase of the brain rewiring, having no doubt as far as you can say that you have the success you need before you see any outcomes supporting that conviction. When you get your mind to that degree of certainty and conviction, you have effectively rewired your brain to accomplish maximum prosperity.

Are you stuck in the "fight or flight" stress reaction during a difficult breakup? Discover how persistent stress over lost love, lost security, or a lost dream may rewire your brain, change your conduct, and leave you defenseless against genuine sickness. Then figure out how to utilize a basic tool that beats stress.

<u>What are the health dangers of breakup stress?</u>

Restorative analysts have proven that persistent stress can raise your pulse, harden arteries, harm your immune system, and elevate your risks of diabetes, Alzheimer's disease, and depression.

Persistent breakup stress can also rewire the brain to promote a vicious cycle of destructive and habitual behavior. What are the signs?

Have you experienced wild, negative feelings or repetitive thoughts about your lost love?

Do you remain awake at nights plotting approaches to avenge a betrayal or broken promises?

Do you fanatically call, email, or stalk your ex?

Do you quit eating or overindulge in food, drug, alcohol, or any physical joy conveyed to a promiscuous excess?

Do you ever feel you don't recognize yourself or your new habits, yet you can't switch back to positive, objective coordinated behaviors?

Now there's new logical proof that these negative practices become a propensity quicker when you're stressed.

Dr. Sapolsky told the New York Times that we are lousy at perceiving when our typical ways of dealing with stress aren't working. Our reaction is to accomplish something multiple times more, rather than thinking this isn't working so perhaps I should be able to do something differently.

How do you utilize this news?

These discoveries may assist you with seeing how an excellent attribute like perseverance can be taken to extreme, uncontrollable repetition and become an unreasonable propensity rapidly under incessant stress.

Breakup stress is regularly constant while you endure a custody battle or divorce, or you grieve the death of a relationship.

If you're stuck in a trench of stress and wild negative propensities, how do you break out of it?

Luckily the brain is a strong and plastic organ.

Dr. Bruce S. McEwen, leader of the brain examination lab at Rockefeller University, told the New York Times that his discoveries show that the brain's dendrites and neural retract and reform, and reversible displaying can happen all through our lifetime.

How did he reach these findings?

Dr. McEwen's exploration group detailed that lab rats exposed to ceaseless stress stayed hyperactive, stuck of negative practices until they got the antidote.

They got a multi-week excursion from these stressors and remained in a supportive setting.

According to Dr. McEwen, the brain is flexible. It settles on new synaptic associations in the decision making districts of the pre-frontal cortex, while the dendrite vines of habit-prone sensorimotor striatum retreat.

How do these discoveries in lab rats help us?

We now understand that incessant stress changes your brain, and relaxation in a supportive domain can transform it.

How can you benefit by relaxation when you're excessively worried by your breakup?

If you can't take a four-week get-away, you can decide to make time to utilize a relaxation device every day.

Do some deep breathing, in a perfect world during a walk in nature.

Listen to relaxation tapes as opposed to taking a stimulating drink break.

Sign up for a progression of therapeutic massages and biofeedback sessions that facilitate your stressful enthusiastic patterns.

Listening to hypnosis audios that diminish stress, helps you reach forgiveness, healing, and recuperating feelings of confidence and peace.

Look for comfort in your confidants, your supportive loved ones.

This activity plan will assist you with enduring a breakup and thrive in your recent single life.

Also, if you're single and seeking supportive companions or master advice to help you start fresh and love once more, enjoy a free months membership in the Singles Club in "Tribe Of Blondes." Not a hair shading, it's resilient positive thinking that joins us and fills our passionate decisions and individual triumphs. Singles club was made by Hadley Finch, author of the novel, "Tribe Of Blondes." It was enlivened by her genuine experiences in starting fresh and discovering love online after her long marriage finished in divorce.

Now, Hadley helps singles with getting a charge out of an all-encompassing recuperation from lost love and quest for new love in a supportive community of savvy singles, affectionately called the Tribe Of Singles.

# Chapter 7

# HOW TO REWIRE YOUR BRAIN FOR SUCCESS

**The brain captivates and keeps me inquisitive.**

Being a trainer, I'm intrigued about the effect of learning on the brain: I'm a big supporter of brain-based and accelerated learning, focused on making an environment where all can learn. The more I dig deep, the more I wish the brain would give up its privileged insights, a little, at least in my lifetime.

Thinking back over the brain studies in the past century, it's astonishing what was once taken as truth is presently classed as complete baloney. I can't accept how we treated the brain. For individuals encountering emotional health illness in the past century, this 'treatment' was awful.

Did You Know This... The Taub Therapy Clinic (University of Birmingham, Alabama) has been exploring and treating individuals who have encountered a stroke with CI Therapy (Constraint Inducement Therapy.)

In short: they have been treating individuals who have had a stroke by 'debilitating' their great limbs or tying them down (well, it's most likely more therapeutic than 'tying'!)

Also, the outcome is: the seriously harmed (note: I utilized harmed, not broken) brain starts to re-wire and re-boot itself, the brain finds an explores an alternate course with the goal that the individual starts to utilize the limbs influenced by the stroke.

Researchers found that by denying the person the ability to get to their 'great' limbs expanded the odds of the brain finding an alternate pathway...a rewire!

On the side which is restricted in development, everything is still in working order (it's all set), but the sign or messages from the brain are not getting through due to the damage left by the stroke.

I can't imagine how disappointing that must be for the individual, however, the best part is the Taub Centers achievement rate, which is a shocking 95%!

Why Tie Up the 'Great' Limbs?

It's direct, our brains constantly take the easiest course!

I didn't say the most 'consistently, the most advantageous course to you,' I said the easiest!

The easiest course for the individual who has had a stroke is the pathways presently working or the most grounded wiring.

(As a trainer, this is amazing, it's another incredible case of the saying, 'Use It, or Lose It.')

What's more, this 'easy way' isn't simply happening to individuals who have had a stroke, brains look for the easiest and simplest route...all the time!

Here's An A-ha Moment.

Could this be the motivation behind why we can compose our objectives effectively, however, achieving them is (for the most part) viewed as harder than thinking of them down? For what reason do a few of us start an objective or go down a particular way of action and rapidly depend on the old habits and behaviors?

What's required?

A re-wiring in the brain, closing down the old ways, and starting up new ones.

How though?

We'll get to that...

For instance: imagine somebody who is sitting in a vehicle and hasn't learned how to drive. They know it all works, but it can't be driven because their brain has not made any 'wiring' on how to drive a vehicle!

The brain needs to become familiar with the knowledge first, wire it in (associate every one of the spots) deep, at exactly that point the brain will learn how to drive and send messages to the various parts of the body, guiding it.

What about someone who has to define an objective to lose weight: they realize it can be done, they have the power, assets, and ability. (They have most likely evidence, a piece of the wiring set up already if they have been around somebody who has shed pounds.)

Why do many resort back to overeating? Because the brain has not rewired itself, the easiest course is to eat!

<u>What about fear?</u> Again, (I would say) most of us do everything to maintain a strategic distance from the things we fear the most, which bodes well, we have to deconstruct the old wiring first!

The strange thing is we all realize that to deconstruct the wiring of the fear, is to do what you fear the most!

<u>Why?</u> You'll make a new way (new program), you'll be rewiring your brain.

<u>What about changing careers?</u> Again many take the least demanding route...they do what's easiest or generally comfortable, not because they won't be able to accomplish something different, but because we haven't made another pathway.

Which is why many change 'work' and not a career! Same crap, diverse backdrop!

Is this why our confidence levels go here and there. We have wiring of where we are confident and where we aren't. The objective is to make the way surest to you, the most grounded, making a pathway so solid it supersedes all others.

The prevailing wiring must be you, being the most confident you.

Consider this profoundly, you can see this occurring all over the place...

For certain people, shedding pounds or losing weight, they may make a big step (maybe Gastric Bypass Surgery) and remove from their life the most effortless course (eating), in doing so , the brain needs to re-wire itself.

For certain individuals subject to alcohol and drugs, they evacuate the most effortless course (simple access to substances) and maybe live for quite a long time in an environment where they are illegal to use.

What about a life brimming with fear? Fears are unique to the individual and can cover a huge number of fears. I've been working with somebody recently who is scared of failing to be loved by another. How does that become rewired? We can't make or demand someone to love us: however, we can re-wire the fear?

Shouldn't something be said about the fear of never 'making a big deal about their life, dying with lament,' can that be re-wired?

The inner feelings of trepidation, constraining idea patterns, habits, and beliefs are harder to re-wire?

I need to state no, they aren't harder.

Whatever we want to re-wire, we should remember that the brain loves the simplest course. To transform anything, the most straightforward course is to state 'it's simply too hard to re-wire,' we presumably wouldn't state that, it would more so be 'I attempted to, however, it didn't work' or 'I failed' or perhaps 'I'm just not good enough.'

<u>Make New Pathways. How?</u>

You can utilize counseling, hypnosis, coaching, CBT, NLP?

Discovering somebody who doesn't have similar wiring as you? (The more you affirm that your wiring is right, the more grounded it gets, making it harder to re-wire. Have you not loved somebody without a doubt, friends unveiled to you they didn't either and before you know it, you detest them with a passion.)

We all realize that the least demanding approach to overcome fear and anxiety is to do what we fear the most, similar to the people above who had experienced a stroke, their treatment must have caused such torment. However, they gave themselves no choice but to push through the agony and fear

Here's an idea...

To deconstruct anything, it's essentially an instance of dismantling it, piece by piece:

Take one of your fears:

- What proof do you have that the dread/fear is wired?

- Picture yourself solving the fear you once had effectively.

- Keep playing the image again and again.

- Only observe, feel, think, be successful.

What's happening with you? Re-wiring. Laying the new track.

Are you prepared to make and craft for yourself an enabled life? Need to reboot your brain for progress? Is it accurate to say that you are prepared to develop self-esteem and confidence, become focused, and push ahead?

# Chapter 8

# REWIRE YOUR BRAIN TO CHANGE EMOTIONAL HABITS

Is your brain being seriously genuinely unhelpful? Would you like it to be entirely rebuilt to be sensible, sane, and not inclined to sobbing madly when you see a little dog? You may be lucky, but just in the broadest of terms. We're progressively understanding that the adult brain is fit for physical change and rewiring in response to stimuli. However, if you think about the brain as an enormously unpredictable series of wires and computer connections, we're still basically pampered with a Fisher-Paykel chisel, slamming at the circuit board.

There are two broadly acknowledged approaches to physically "rewire" the emotional responses and brain's associations: careful contemplation, and psychological behavioral treatment. Mindfulness is a type of treatment that empowers exceptional self-awareness of the mind on the planet; for instance, OCD patients trained to be mindful of their violent thoughts in a research showed both apparent changes and a huge improvement in their neural connections. Intellectual behavioral treatment is a remedial technique that challenges and effectively tries to supplant negative speculation patterns in the brain, and in the process seems to physically move the structure of the brain. However, beyond these, more readily open strategies (you can get CBT from numerous specialists, and mindfulness practice is even accessible through YouTube instructional exercises), can science be able to assist us with going further in moving the structure of our brains in helpful manners?

The appropriate response is: yes, within points of confinement. Various logical research has shown ways by which the brain can be changed without the requirement for a lobotomy. We should take an emotional journey.

## 1. Comprehend Your Brain's Plasticity

A lot of work on the adult brain in recent decades has added to a move in a key conviction: that our brains are a fixed unit when we hit our 30s. We are continuously finding that isn't the situation, upsetting a great deal of acknowledged considering the brain and its abilities simultaneously. In case you will effectively change your brain, first, you have to see how neuroplasticity, as it's called, really works.

Neuroplasticity is fundamentally "the capacity [of the brain] to change its structure and function in light of experience," as Sharon Begley of TIME set it back in 2007 when a large group of new studies were emerging about brain shifts. It's especially clear in the brain's physical rewiring when it or the body suffers damage, frequently making compensatory links to attempt to get a move on in territories of the brain that used to be dedicated to different things. The brain's physical organization can modify in light of necessities and experiences, which implies that if you change your experiences and needs, you can change your brain.

Not so fast. Scientific American in 2014 sounded a note of warning: the brain is a tremendously complex organ, regardless of huge leaps forward by the way we comprehend and imagine its activity. They focused on "brain games" that intend to utilize neuroplasticity to improve things like memory and spatial capacity; for reasons unknown, we're still not educated enough about the (extremely explicit) systems that govern those things to be able to fiddle with them. You can't simply go out to change your brain in helpful ways.

### 2.  "Fire Together, Wire Together"

The one thing we do think about as it regards neurobiology is that there often seem to be a "fire together, wire together" rule at play. At the end of the day, if certain neurons continue firing simultaneously, in the long run, they'll build up a physical association and get physically related as well. It's called experience-dependent plasticity, regardless we're learning the exact ways in which it changes our brains, however, it's essentially similar to repeating a decent habit.

A famous report referred by Berkeley's Greater Good foundation considered the brains of London taxi drivers, who'd needed to retain the city's layout by heart, and discovered they had extremely thick associations in their visual-spatial cortex. If you work on something reliably, at the end of the day, you're probably going to adjust your brain to relate the pertinent pieces of its structure.

This specific thought is at the foundation of a lot of research on rewiring our emotional reactions and helping us be more joyful. The psychologist, Rick Hanson, in an interview with the Huffington Post on the standard, proposed endeavoring to acknowledge, practice, and truly implant cheerful experiences in the mind, to get the brain to wire more genuinely positive responses. This isn't new-age gibberish, either; various research has indicated that probable for transformative reasons, the brain responds unmistakably more strongly to negative experiences than to positive ones, and experience training might be a method for fixing this intrinsic "negativity bias." We're still uncertain about the exact neural examples that could react to this treatment, however, there's no damage in being aware of your happiness.

**Let MIT Researchers Rewire Your Emotional Memory**

Alright, this one is not a thing to attempt at home, however, it's interesting. In 2014, MIT researchers uncovered that they'd figured out how to control the memories of mice to change their emotional affiliations. To do it, however, they physically changed the neurons firing in the brain (they did it utilizing a method called optogenetics, which uses light to modify the capacity of neurons, in case you're intrigued).

The researchers fundamentally turned pleasant and unpleasant memories on and off in the brains of mice utilizing their neural light-switch and discovered they could move the emotional relationship with the memories in the mice's brains. Mice who'd been adapted to associate something with fear could be changed to associating it with decent stuff, and once more, absolutely through actuating a specific piece of the brain. I don't prescribe letting an MIT researcher get into your head with optogenetics (who am I kidding? That sounds cool), however, this might be the fate of genuine therapy for treating individuals with traumatic memories, for instance.

1. **Stay away from Stress And Its Tendency To Make Habits Fixed**

We're discovering progressively that stress does something very fascinating for the brain: it digs inhabits. A 2009 research on rodents found that, under constant stress, they were substantially more liable to depend on automatic decisions (decisions we make simply through habit) than cognizant ones they'd unmistakably thought through. Their brain composition also changed to reflect this. The researchers behind this revelation contemplate brain energy: during genuine stress, the brain will take the easiest way, and consume as little energy possible on deciding, so it'll return to habits.

It's significant to remember that positive emotions aren't the main ones that can rewire the brain; negative ones like stress and anxiety can have genuine effects as well. Along with the development of dangerous habits, it can likewise shape abnormal associations. A fascinating research found that on edge or troubling circumstances brief the brain to rewire its associations with the olfactory centers (the parts that process smell), giving negative or sickening association to smells that are regularly observed as very neutral. Indeed, that is the reason your ex boyfriend previously delicious cologne currently smells like death.


## 2.  Do A Specific Brain-Training Task

In a fascinating research discharged in 2016, a little set of test subjects seemed to uncover that a specific brain-training task does a touch of rewiring of the brain's emotional centers. The undertaking was about ignoring irrelevant information: the 26 participants needed to state which direction an arrow pointed while disregarding arrows on either side of it. Training that develops the ability to neglect unimportant information can accomplish lessened mind response to enthusiastic events and modify brain connections joined by fortified neural associations between brain regions engaged with repressing emotional responses," as indicated by the researchers liable for the investigation. Individuals who'd experienced extreme bolt tests had a lower measure of enactment in their amygdala, which is associated with emotions, and a greater association between the amygdala and a territory of the brain related to passionate regulation. Essentially, their brains were progressively ready to overlook negative emotions. It was a small study and the impacts were just concentrated in a truly transient manner, however, if it's true, it's entrancing.

Do-it-yourself brain rewiring may be available in the market sooner or later, however, for the time being, it would seem that your best bet is thinking positively, doing mindful reflection, taking up treatment, and remaining as far away from stress as could be expected under the circumstances. So, generally good ideas, then.

## Do you Appear to Get Caught up in the Same Old Reactions?

Have you at any point blown up at your life partner just to acknowledge - after the smoke cleared - that you may have over-reacted only a smidgen? Perhaps you discover that you haven't been invited to your uncle's companion's sister's birthday party and you carry on as though it's the slight of the century. Sometimes even the most minor disaster can send us raging out of the room, hammering down a telephone, or simply closing down completely. It's like we can't resist - the response is as programmed as a mallet to the knee.

## Research Says You May Not Be At Fault

New research shows that these routine, knee-jerk reactions traces back to our youth. As youths, we figured out how to adjust to our families' characteristics as a method for endurance. Analysts used to allude to these methods for dealing with stress as our effects – however, what science has now indicated to us is that these reactions are in reality hard-wired into our brains. Also, because our reactions are so instilled, they have become our sifting system for future incidents. As such, if something happens today that the brain reads as being like something that occurred before, it will react as though it were the first time, although you might be in your 30's, 40's, 50's, 60's and beyond.

## Bringing This to Life

For instance, suppose a kid comes from a home where the guardians fight now and again. That kid is going to connect hollering with terrible emotions. In later years, if his life partner raises her voice, he's probably going to shut down like when he was a child - allegorically hurrying to his room, shutting the door, and blocking out the noise.

Does this mean if you come from a family of yellers you're bound to cover up under your bed each time somebody raises a voice? Fortunately, ongoing research shows that the brain keeps on developing for the duration of our lives, and old patterns can be discharged as new ones are framed in your boomer years.

## Help Is On the Way

The best approach to dealing with your knee jerk and anger responses is to build up new associations by refocusing your consideration to a different possibility or outcome. But, before you can cultivate these new connections in your brain, you must know about the old brain triggers.

When I try to recognize whether somebody's response is a past association, I hope to check whether their response to the circumstance is programmed and extraordinary. Moreover, when I try and offer an alternative to why they're behaving that way, the individual is reluctant and resistant to think about some other view or translation of the circumstance - other than their own.

Here is a simple exercise to kick you off on rewiring your brain to control your outrage and over-reactions that will realize positive changes throughout your life today!

**Considering Alternatives:**

**a.** When you're projecting your experience onto a present one, try to imagine possible approaches to deal with the circumstance. For instance, suppose you have lunch plans with a friend - who cancels at the last minute. Immediately, you feel an overwhelming feeling of rejection and hurt. Which is how you generally feel in comparative circumstances - showing - voila - a past pattern! Be aware of this and take a step back to recognize it.

**b.** At that point, approach the circumstance from a completely alternate point of view. Perhaps you use humor to deflect the bad emotions, thinking to yourself, "Well, I get it's my deodorant." Or, you choose the direct approach and inquire as to whether you've done something to upset her. Or on the other hand, you take the practice route and figure your friend just overbooked, overextended, or over-guaranteed - and give her an escape prison free card. (Hint: If you experience issues coming up with alternative approaches to deal with the circumstance, consider how another person - your mom, a cherished friend, a respected colleague - might deal with a similar circumstance.)

**Plugging in New Choices:**

**a.** Now, replay the genuine circumstance as distinctively as possible - the telephone ringing, the sound of your friend's voice, the awkward farewells - and imagine yourself doing one of your new solutions. Perhaps you conclude that being understanding of your friend's busy timetable is the best choice.

**b.** Replay the telephone call and plug in your new behavior, the understanding you, instead of playing out your old conduct of feeling rejected and hurt.

**Making it Last**

Before long, you will start to see a slight move in the way you feel. By doing this activity over and over, you will pull together your attention to another result. This will rewire your brain and make another neural connection – a connection to positive change!

# Chapter 9

# REWIRE YOUR BRAIN TO DEVELOP HEALTHY HABITS

If you have ever attempted to avoid that pizza at the staff party at work, you realize what a challenge it is to keep your fingers out of the case and rather go for the salad that nobody has touched. Ohh and once you get to that salad, the battle isn't finished. Indeed, even at your work area, you continue contemplating that stunning combo of sauce, dough, and cheese…

What makes it so challenging to disregard that slice? You deal with yourself by believing that it extends a little piece.. you'll just have one… but will it help you reach your goal? The fight is going on in your mind… and it has an inseparably tied to mindset and habits.

## COMFORTABLE HABITS

The magnet that pulls you toward that pizza goes way pass only a mild interest: it feels like your impulse to want it and leaving feels incomprehensible.

When you taste foods that are easily worth craving (things that are sugary, fatty, or salty), your brain releases chemicals into circulation that tells you "hey this feels good." At that moment we feel pleasure and maybe we forget about things that aren't so nice for a minute. This effect has been described by experts to mimic, to some degree, what a smoker feels when they light up or even what a heroin user feels when they get high. For some that addiction to food may be so great that changing this behavior can feel hopeless.

The great vibe that you can get from food is the thing for many that take that feeling away.

That "great vibes" originates from a compound created and discharged by a few territories of your brain called dopamine. Your body loves dopamine and it will fool you into doing almost anything to get some of it streaming around within you. The reason you want to eat up slice after slice is because you furtively need dopamine to go through you and that pizza will get you there. Your body recalls how great it tasted and how magnificent it makes you feel. Dopamine motivates you to focus on that slice and dopamine motivates you to place your hand in the crate/box.

Now your body says, "Hello that felt better... so why don't we do it once more?" Your brain is currently wired to need that pizza. Think about anything else, you don't just have the box sitting before you for your body to be reminded about dopamine... have you at any point made an uncommon outing to the store for a snack that you simply needed to have right at that point? That is your body recalling how that bite gave you a portion of that sweet dopamine.

## THE SAD NEWS

Unfortunately, most Americans (an estimated 160 million) are either overweight or obese. This incorporates almost 75% of American men and over 60% of American ladies. These are likewise significant difficulties for America's kids – almost 30% of boys and girls under age 20 are either overweight or obese, up from 19% in 1980. The strain this puts on things like social insurance costs and charges on the American individuals, in general, is unbelievable.

Our way of life breeds this conduct. We are immersed in promotions for quick and processed foods, soda, candy, alcohol life in abundance. Our general public is broad with these kinds of impacts and imbues us into accepting that we need to live with these things in our lives. Wherever we turn, we are bombarded not just with unhealthy food and we are left with brains that, whenever wired to do as such, drive us to want it.

## HOWEVER, THERE IS HOPE

Now there is a promising end of the tunnel: you can rewire your brain and change the way that you are on. With some persistence and an honest desire to transform, you can be discharged from the grip that unhealthy foods have over you. You can change your point of view and all the while, pass by the pizza box, driving you to a significantly more noteworthy prize.

The puzzle is illuminated by changing your mindset. It's an acknowledgment of what is progressively critical to you. You have to need great health, a superior body, more years with your grandchildren, the ability to run a long-distance race, or whatever else you can consider more than that cut of additional cheese. Anything more noteworthy than your craving if anything you have to make sense of. Find that thing that is increasingly critical to you and put it before you. At work, at home. Constantly.. everywhere. Your "significant thing" should give your body all the dopamine it is longing for, both while endeavoring to accomplish it and when you do. Always remember, if you can't resist that slice of pizza, your "significant thing" probably won't be as significant as you thought.

## ALRIGHT, I KNOW WHAT'S SIGNIFICANT TO ME. SO NOW WHAT?

When you've discovered your "significant thing" that will supplant your undesirable dietary patterns, how will you remain on track?

### Be a pioneer and defend your objective.

When you start, this will be a challenge, however, you should expel yourself from things that inspire poor choices. When everybody around you is guzzling soda and shoving fistfuls of birthday cake into their mouths, you will struggle. You will be in the genuinely charged circumstance and your body will need to join the gathering when perhaps your psyche won't. Place your "significant thing" at the front of your mind and ask yourself whether that glass of Mountain Dew will assist you with arriving at your objectives. Consider where you will be if you continue making good decisions.

### Be proud of your achievements.

When you get an accomplishment, you will have achieved significantly more than trying to say no to an unhealthy decision. Guess what else.. your body likes accomplishments as well! Ride that wave. Like your success. You have ventured out rewiring your brain to habitual patterns. Much the same as working out, you get a little more grounded without fail. Each time it'll get somewhat simpler.

## Keep Going

Accomplish your "significant thing?" Great! Locate another one. As you rewire your brain, you are making new habits that, sooner or later, will be a lot more grounded than the "shove this pizza in your mouth" ones. Ensure that any "significant thing" that you picked is additionally healthy – don't take up smoking to kick pop. Your "significant thing" ought to have esteem that can apply to the individuals who you care about or encompass you. It ought to be something that rushes, stimulates, and motivates you to develop.

Overthinking may be something you need to train your brain to quit doing, particularly if it causes issues for you. For instance, does your overthinking lead to a negative state of mind or increase your level of anxiety? Does it prevent you from doing things that you have to complete? Are you hesitating to settle on a choice since you need to weigh the entirety of the potential results?

Overthinking can have negative ramifications for the individuals who are incessant worriers. Concentrating on future uncertainties makes us restless when we feel an absence of control. Overthinking can likewise prevent us from getting a charge out of the present moment. We should investigate approaches to train your brain to quit overthinking and start acknowledging what is here for us in the now.

Researchers at the University of California at Santa Barbara showed images of kaleidoscope colors to study members and then tested their ability to remember if they had seen an image previously. Members who took their best guess at the memory test did better than those who spent time trying to remember colors and patterns. The overthinkers focused their brainpower on recalling the visual information that they were presented with did less well than those who did not focus on recalling details.

The specialists say that this study shows 'why focusing can be a distraction and influence execution results.' The region of the brain in our prefrontal cortex that is dynamic when we focus is the dorsolateral zone. Members with less prefrontal cortex stimulation during the test recalled the pictures better. As such, giving more consideration to details hurt their capacity to recall what they had seen.

The research shows that an increasingly expansive diagram approach might be better for reviewing complex pictures. To prepare your brain to process data along these lines, attempt to envision taking in all of the details at once, as if your brain is taking a picture and seeing all of the snippets of information without a moment's delay.

You can work on underthinking by finding an image book, opening to a random page, and taking a look at a picture for five seconds. Close the book and attempt to review everything that you saw. The short measure of time keeps your brain from overthinking, however, you will be amazed at how much you can recall. Attempt this over and over until you feel increasingly positive about your brain's capacity to process data rapidly.

## Train your Brain to Be Comfortable with Unpredictability

There are things you can know, and things you may never know. Overthinkers have prepared their brains to concentrate on the vulnerabilities since they are attempting to explain them. For an overthinker, their brain resembles that of a multi-year old always looking for answers. Although a few questions can be answered, overthinkers may will in general dwell on those that can't.

Or possibly they figure they can't be answered, for instance 'What could they possibly have implied when they said that?' could be effectively answered by requesting that the person clarify their meaning. 'I wonder what they think of me?' could be answered by asking the individual whose supposition you are overthinking. Either seek the answer to the question that you are overthinking, or advise your brain that you'll have to be okay with not knowing the appropriate response.

## Train Your Brain To Observe Your Negativity

Meta-thinking is considering how you think, which requires some self-perception. In case you're reading this book and have concerns about your overthinking, you are now aware of your inefficient reasoning patterns. Individuals who experience trouble with overthinking usually have negative considerations about themselves as a result of their thoughts.

Enabling negative contemplations to exist while dismissing them as being a piece of what we distinguish as 'self' is a part of a strategy that can support overthinkers. Scientists in the journal Behavior Therapy found that care based psychological treatment (MBCT) helped individuals to feel more self-sympathy instead of negative feelings about their overthinking. Individuals who experienced MBCT treatment experienced less stress-related to their thoughts.

**Discover One Thing You Can Control**

If overthinking is going on because you have to gain control over a circumstance, at that point discover one solid step that you can do to restore some feeling of control. For instance, writing down the issue is basic and it enables your brain to quit attempting to recall the issue. Then recognize one more thing you can do that will be a step in the right decision, for instance, making a telephone call to get more information.

# Chapter 10

# THE TEN FUNDAMENTALS OF REWIRING YOUR BRAIN

Neuroplasticity has become a trendy expression in scientific and psychology circles, just as outside of them, promising that you can rewire your mind to improve everything from health and mental prosperity to personal satisfaction. There's a great deal of clashing, misleading, and erroneous information out there.

## What is Neuroplasticity?

Just in case you've figured out how to miss all the publicity, neuroplasticity is an umbrella term alluding to the capacity of your brain to rearrange itself, both physically and practically, throughout your life due to your environment, emotions, thinking, and behavior. The idea of neuroplasticity isn't new and mentions of a moldable brain go all of the way back to the 1800s. With the generally new ability to "see" into the brain permitted by functional magnetic reverberation imaging (fMRI), science has affirmed the extraordinary morphing ability of the brain without question.

The idea of a changing brain has supplanted the previously held conviction that the adult brain was practically a physiologically static organ or hard-wired, after basic formative periods in childhood. While it is the truth that your brain is significantly more plastic during the early years and limit decreases with age, plasticity happens all through your life.

## How Neuroplasticity Shows Up in Your Life

Neuroplasticity makes your brain amazingly flexible and is the procedure by which all lasting learning happens in your brain, for example, playing an instrument or acing an alternate language. Neuroplasticity likewise empowers individuals to recoup from stroke, injury, and birth anomalies, defeat chemical imbalance, ADD and ADHD, learning disabilities, and other brain deficiencies, haul out of addictions and sadness and reverse obsessive-compulsive patterns.

Neuroplasticity has extensive ramifications and conceivable outcomes for pretty much every part of human life and culture from education to medicine. Its cutoff points are not yet known. Be that as it may, this same characteristic, which makes your mind incredibly versatile, additionally makes it powerless against outside and inner, normally oblivious, impacts.

I know the intensity of neuroplasticity, as I concocted and played out my very own home-developed, experience-dependent neuroplasticity-based activities for a considerable length of time to recoup from brain damage, the consequence of a suicide attempt. Furthermore, through broad subjective conduct treatment, reflection, and mindfulness practices, all of which encourage neuroplastic change, I conquered anxiety, depression, and improved mental health and life.

It was also a result of a neuroplastic change that I got dug in anxious, depressive, obsessive and over-reactive patterns in the first place.


**Ten Fundamentals of Neuroplasticity**

Science has affirmed that you can get to neuroplasticity for positive change in your life from numerous points of view, however, it's not exactly as simple as some of the neuro-hype would have you believe. Dr. Sarah McKay, neuroscientist, composes:

Plasticity dials back 'ON' in adulthood when explicit conditions that empower or trigger plasticity are met. 'What ongoing exploration has shown is that under the right conditions, the intensity of brain plasticity can help adults' minds develop. Although certain brain machinery will in general decline with age, there are steps individuals can take to tap into plasticity and revitalize that machinery,' explains Merzenich. These conditions incorporate centered consideration, hard work, determination, and maintaining overall brain health.

Dr. Michael Merzenich (which Dr. McKay refers to over), the main pioneer in brain plasticity research and co-founder of Posit Science, records ten core principles important for the redesigning of your brain to happen:

> 1. Change is mostly constrained to those circumstances in which the brain is in the mood for it. If you are alert, motivated,

engaged, on the ball, ready for action, the brain discharges the neurochemicals necessary to empower brain change. When disengaged, distracted, inattentive, or doing something without thinking that requires no genuine exertion, your neuroplastic switches are "off."

2. The harder you attempt, the more you're motivated, the more alarm you are, and the better (or more awful) the potential result, the greater the brain change. In case you're seriously focused around the undertaking and attempting to ace something for a significant reason, the change experienced will be more prominent.

3. What changes in the brain are the qualities of the associations between neurons that are engaged together, minute by minute, in time? The more something is practiced, the more associations are changed and made to incorporate all components of the experience (sensory information, cognitive patterns, movement). You can consider it like an "ace controller" made for that specific behavior which enables it to be performed with amazing facility and dependability over time.

4. Learning-driven changes in associations increment cell-to-cell cooperation which is vital for expanding reliability. Merzenich clarifies this by soliciting you to envision the sound from a football arena brimming with fans all applauding at random versus the same individuals applauding as one. He explains, "The more powerfully coordinated your [nerve cell] teams are, the more powerful and more reliable their behavioral productions."

5. The brain likewise reinforces its associations between teams of neurons representing separate moments of progressive things that dependably happen in sequential time. This procedure enables your brain to anticipate what occurs next and have a persistent "acquainted stream." Without this capacity, your stream of consciousness would be decreased to "a progression of independent, stagnating puddles," Merzenich explains.

6. Initial changes are impermanent. Your brain first records the change, at that point decides if it should roll out the improvement perpetual or not. It possibly becomes permanent if your brain decides the experience to be captivating or novel enough or if the social result is significant, good, or bad.

7. The brain is changed by inner mental practice in similar ways and including precisely similar procedures that control changes accomplished through connections with the outer world. As per Merzenich, "You don't need to move an inch to drive positive plastic change in your brain. Your inward representations of things reviewed from memory work fine for dynamic brain plasticity-based learning."

8. Memory controls and guides must be learned. As you get familiar with another aptitude, your brain observes and recalls the great endeavors, while disposing of the bad ones. Then it reviews the last great situation, makes steady modifications, and logically improves.

9. Each movement of learning gives a moment of opportunity to the brain to balance out - and diminish the problematic intensity of - conceivably interfering foundations or "commotion." Each time your brain fortifies an association to advance your mastery of a skill, it additionally debilitates other connections of neurons that weren't utilized at that exact minute. This negative plastic brain change deletes a portion of the interfering or irrelevant activity in the brain.

10. Brain plasticity is a two-way road. It's equally as simple to produce negative changes as positive ones. It's nearly as simple to drive changes that debilitate memory and physical and mental capacities for what it's worth to improve these things. Merzenich says that more seasoned individuals are absolute masters at empowering plastic brain-altering in an inappropriate course.

# Chapter 11

# OPTIMIZE YOUR BRAIN – PRACTICE MINDFULNESS

Collectively and individually, we have been navigating a particular stressful timeframe in our local and worldwide economy. There seem to be constant reports of worldwide and neighborhood political agitation, climate challenges, and natural disaster notwithstanding the struggling economy. I don't think about you, but I have felt the heaviness of this on my spirit each time I turn on the news, read papers, and listen to my customers talk about their circumstances and the circumstances of their companions and family members.

There might be no preferred time over now for an exercise in mindfulness to assist people with enhancing brain function, decline anxiety, and figure out how to live in the now. With such a great amount of vulnerability in our lives, the one thing we can control is where we put our thought. Things being what they are, where we concentrate matters a lot to how our brain and how we regulate our moods.

Let me start by giving you a working definition of "mindfulness" as characterized by Jon Kabat-Zinn, the author of "Mindfulness-Based Stress Reduction." Kabat-Zinn said that mindfulness is, "paying attention on purpose."

This is a decent sounding definition, however, it does little to portray how and why (when and where) we can practice mindfulness, so how about we unload it a piece. First off, you can practice mindfulness pretty much anytime and anywhere. The minute that you understand your body or brain is feeling the effect of negative emotions (stress, outrage, hurt, bitterness, hopelessness, and so on) you can start to check out the present minute by monitoring how and where you are holding the feelings.

Notice where in your body you are feeling the effect of the negative emotion. Start to breathe deeply in and out, through the nose, and give close consideration to how the breathing feels in your lungs and body. Connect with your psyche completely in the breathing procedure for snappy access to the present minute. Move your contemplations and thoughtfulness regarding the vibe of the sun (rain, cold, warmth, or some other component) on your skin. Note how this feels - the warmth on your skin, the bright light (of the sun) sifting through your eyelids. Return your attention to your breathing whenever your mind starts to meander away from the present minute.

Another method for becoming mindful is to just watch your very own perception procedure. It may sound something like this in your brain, "I feel my stomach rise when I breathe deeply which makes me feel the waistband of my jeans when my stomach expands. I notice the solidness of the fabric of my jeans and as I feel the texture, I notice how my eyes want to take a look at what I am feeling, and now I can see that my jeans are faded blue with wrinkles to a great extent. I can also feel my curiosity provoke about the little darker spot I see on my jeans."

It turns into a running dialogue in your psyche as you become aware of and connected with your senses and how they are taking in your environment. When a judgment of your perceptions attempts to embed itself, just hear or see the judging idea, let it cross and move out of your thoughts and re-center around your breath. Become your very own empathetic observer of your own emotions and thoughts.

<u>Here is a related snippet from a research study:</u>

A research conducted by the University of Pennsylvania in which training was given to a high-stress U.S. military group planning for deployment to Iraq has shown a positive connection between mindful training, or MT, and enhancements in mood and working memory. Mindfulness is the ability to know and be aware of the present minute without emotional reactivity or instability.

This study found that the additional time members spent taking an interest in a type of everyday mindfulness training (MT) exercises, the better their state of mind and working memory became. The study additionally exhibited that adequate MT practice may secure against functional weaknesses related to high-stress difficulties that require a huge measure of psychological control, emotional guideline, and self-awareness." (This snippet was taken from "Mindfulness Helps Mood and Memory" by Tyler Woods, Ph.D.).

Similarly, as physical exercise performed daily enables the body to become more healthy and more grounded, practicing mindfulness day by day helps the brain (physical brain and the mind) become stronger and healthier.

As a therapist, I have discovered that individuals experience anxiety when they are either pondering the past (ruminating) or thinking (stressing) about what's to come. The main time we ought to be thinking about the future is the point at which we are taking part in problem-solving, objective setting, and action-oriented planning. The main time we ought to consider the past is the point at which we need to pick up something explicit about what our history can teach us and how we can utilize our history to recuperate, to make new opportunities, and to practice forgiveness (toward our self or others).

Get into a new and wonderful habit and utilize your breath, your mind-body mindfulness, your immediate environment, and your perception procedures to turn out to be progressively mindful and to rewire your brain for vitality and health.

In boxing, there is an idiom that says all boxers have a plan until they get hit. I love that saying since it represents superbly my past fights with anxiety side effects. At the point when I start feeling better, I generally make a plan about what I will do to control my anxiety, however, when my anxiety symptoms hit, my plan would always fall apart as though Mike Tyson himself punched me square on the nose. That continued until I found another plan.

To control your anxiety, you must have a plan. What I mean by a plan is an approach to sort out a genuine set of thoughts or actions processes to assist you with adapting to your anxiety symptoms when they hit you like a padded sack of blocks. The plan can vary from one person to another because no one approach will work for everybody. However, I may want to highlight a procedure that I utilize constantly. It's not a secret, it involves no medications and best of all it's free. To control your anxiety symptoms viably, you need to complete two things. You need to practice these two things again and again for a long time and perhaps months - but it will enable you to adapt. I offer no cures because I am hesitant to ensure the unguaranteeable, however, I will say that if you give it a try, it will assist you with reducing your anxiety at the very least and may even put your anxiety on break.

First and foremost, you need to acknowledge and give up. That is right, it is simple, but after looking into it further, this is in reality, very difficult. You need to acknowledge your anxiety symptoms 100% and not include any more anxiety and stress when your symptoms are activated. You see when we have a panic attack or other anxiety-related symptoms, it hits us hard, and when it does, this creates a lot of fear and worry about us having the symptom (fear or fear). As such, you get a symptom and pump up the fear/dread since you are startled by the symptom. You crank up the intensity and what began as a passing feeling of anxiety or tension can be transformed into an all-out D day attack on your nerves.

What you should do is acknowledge whatever your body and mind will do and not worry when it occurs. So if you are lightheaded, dizzy, have muscle twitches, pains, aches, or have a huge headache, I say so what. These indications won't hurt you. You should acknowledge every one of them regardless of how strong. Try not to add any anxiety or fear to your state.

Ride it and don't give it any significance. Loosen yourself in your seat, stand calmly, whatever your position don't waiver. Allow the anxiety attack as it likes, and don't shrink from it. If you avoid adding extra or secondary fear of the symptoms, your body will normally relax after a short time. Why is this significant? Simply put, you need to re-train your brain and body to not overreact to symptoms and sensations.

You must be firm and in the process, you will rewire your brain. By enabling the anxiety symptoms to go through you and give no extra fear - no 'what if' - you are training your mind and body to not produce anxiety about being anxious. When you do commit the error (we all have) of adding this auxiliary fear, 'the what if,' this is precisely when your anxiety symptoms develop outside your ability to control. The body will discharge adrenaline and keep on fomenting your mind and organs. It is an awful cycle of anxiety - secondary fear - adrenaline – more anxiety. Stop the cycle by removing the continued overproduction of adrenaline. This is the reason you should acknowledge and give up. Of all the days and nights that you have endured anxiety symptoms how often have they harmed you physically? Your likely answer was zero. In this way, be sure and realize that if you don't add more dread to the main case of tension it will pass sooner and extra time you will have less fewer attacks of anxiety symptoms.

Second, you should be patient and enable time to do the rest. If you gain enough practice, you will turn out to be great at the art of sitting idle. No pacing, no rocking, no 'what if' scenarios going through your head. Once more, this may not cure you, but it will give you an idea about your anxiety. With time you will start to feel the band lift from around your head, that lump in your throat will be less perceptible and you will have fewer experiences with your anxious emotions. Is this easy? No, it isn't. However, if you read this and re-read this and then practice you will show signs of improvement. You will recover control.

Therapy and drugs are completely incredible approaches to help you cope with anxiety. However, I firmly believe that the same way you slipped into your restless state is the same way you will get out, which is gradually. You need to acknowledge the palpitations, frail legs, and the other billion and one symptom. If you have been to your primary care physician, possibly a few times, and have been cleared therapeutically then given up. Why worry and battle when you will lose that fight unfailingly. If you don't present a battle, there won't be a battle. Allow yourself to rest, enable the anxiety to do anything it desires. Inevitably you will see the distinction. The anxiety may remain, however, it will stop to linger so enormously in your life. You will still have good and bad days, but this is a genuine technique for adapting and expanding the number of days you feel better. Given the perfect measure of practice, you will have returned to doing what you like to do. You won't want to be locked up in your home. Let go and you will see more promising days.

# Chapter 12

# REWIRED TO WIN

### - Your Competitive Advantage is All in your Mind

People in business- whether in leaderships, employees, or entrepreneurs are motivated to prevail in various manners. In this, they share a great deal in common with those people who practice martial arts. How about we examine and look at these two fields and see precisely what they share in common and can empower you as a success-oriented achiever.

### How are the best business professionals and martial artists alike?

Both practice mental conditioning, consolidating those abilities with their experience and knowledge to successfully reach their objectives. If you are training others, the strengths of martial arts will fabricate their abilities. If you as of now have an effective business, understanding the standards of martial arts and bringing them to bear on your day by day errands could drastically expand your influence and success.

Some of the advantages that business experts gain from martial arts are like the characteristics that individuals associated with both the best martial artists and the best business experts: a ground-breaking presence; an ability to manage emotions under tension; the courage to judiciously handle tough situations, and the ability to adjust to evolving circumstances. When practiced every day, the two disciplines: build resiliency to be able to bounce back from difficulties rapidly; enable you to turn into an agent of change and to coordinate change; refocus your thinking as the circumstance changes; channel your attention to managing the circumstance.

### Martial Arts as a Science and an Art

Martial arts - karate, kick-boxing, tae kwon do, and so on - is both a science and an art. Utilizing it as a science, martial artists train to build up their techniques in figuring out how to situate their hands, feet, and body to perform a punch, execute a turning kick, or dodge a punch or kick without losing their balance. Martial artists practice the various procedures until the feeling of the method and its execution become hard-wired. Utilizing it as an art, they practice much like a dancer, painter, sculptor, or musician- refining their art with everyday best practices to constantly reinforce their muscles, reflexes, and abilities.

It's the equivalent to business experts. The effective ones constantly strengthen their muscles, reflexes, and abilities in the everyday operations of their business. Strong business experts apply their abilities dependent on in-depth studies and research. These incorporate such regions as engaging worker motivation, executing change management, being a pioneer who encapsulates and promotes transformational initiative, running viable meetings, and conveying superb client assistance.

This implies in the art of martial arts and business experts, it takes preparation, training, applying, and coaching what is learned. Through practice, military artists hard-wire their strategies in their brain by persistently sharpening their aptitudes. While genuine business expertise originates from something other than just reading books or taking an interest in a teleclass, business experts hard-wire in their brains what they realize by constantly applying the knowledge so they can act with more confidence, precision, and influence.

## Your competitive benefits start first in your mind

In the book "Hard Optimism," Price Pritchett writes,

"The brain is currently the main productivity tool. Thinking has become the key competency. Individuals' thinking processes are the most significant performance factor."

This implies all human action starts in the brain - an intersection of our ideal results, creative mind, and imagination. Martial artists visualize the desired result and practice successful strategies thousands of times to solidify the wiring between the brain and the body with the goal that it gets programmed. Although various martial arts rules collectively transfer to life and the business world, there are three key standards or mental aptitudes that underlyingly affect business experts and throughout everyday life.

- Awareness

- Mental Toughness
- Focus

Business school, as well as your business experience, showed you these psychological abilities, to a certain extent; the business experts who learn them well and practice them consistently succeed. Whether your fundamental work is driving your business and team – planning, researching, setting goals, and strategizing - or participating actually as a sales rep or active producer - you can utilize these three mental standards to upgrade your performance.

To become a winner in business and life, you should initially become a champ in your brain. However, to change your reasoning, you should first re-wire your brain.

**Re-Wiring Your Brain to Create New Pathways**

Brain specialist, Dr. Jill Ammon-Wesler, in her book, "Zap Your Life: Feel the Power!" composes that,

"Your brain normally blossoms with change and challenge. Current science presently has evidence our brains always develop and change well into old age. The brain is very variable that the logical world needed to make another term - "brain plasticity"....our brains constantly re-wire themselves within hours following each new experience."

What this means to you is that you can re-make yourself, make a new path, and show your desires right there in your brain! Imagine: what might it want to re-wire your brain into the psychological focal point of an Olympic athlete, or to experience business clarity like Bill Gates?

Neurologically, our brains have just been molded by past patterns of thought, attitudes, mood, and emotions. In the womb, our genetic DNA starts assembling our brain and developing certain neurological pathways. After birth, every one of us gets sensory information and various encounters that keep on building our brains. Our responses and reactions to those encounters further build our brains. The soonest, most grounded, and most repetitive encounters - and our reactions - hard-wire our brain.

An example is when little children, who experience issues in understanding cognizance and whose imperfections are persistently called attention to by authority figures, in the long run, develop "profound trenches" of poor self-image and self-esteem - reflected in negative self-talk - which become a significant part of their brain's composition. While they can fabricate new roads through positive reasoning - and set down new pathways and propensities to challenge, diminish, and even defeat negative ones - the old ruts are never erased. Neurological pathways remain, and even new encounters can fall into those old negative ruts of reasoning.

This is a significant idea in understanding how our mind works. One of the general laws of the mind is this: whatever your mind constantly contemplates will often become reality. If for instance, you always feel that your item won't sell, it won't. You have made a psychological desire - your reasoning turns out to be first a rut and afterward a self-fulfilling prophecy.

To rewire your brain and to change this negative result, you should stop the negative idea and train yourself to think differently. What result do you need from them? When you depict the result you need, your perspectives won't just incline toward accomplishing it, but your brain will start thinking through the best possible steps to make the goal a reality.

Imagine a Wall Street ticker tape. Substitute the stock images on the ticker tape for individual contemplations. Similarly, an interminable loop of positive and negative thought circles in our minds. In all actuality, every one of us can intentionally, and deliberately apply exertion to change our thoughts, sort out them into sound patterns, and afterward control how we process those thoughts at any moment. In  martial arts, we are trained not exclusively to control the nature of our reasoning, but in addition to deal with our feelings. This originates from the act of being constantly aware of what we think and how we feel.

For instance, Carla is a new leader at a media transmission organization who is asked by her supervisor to present at an organization meeting. She has presented before to a smaller audience, but this is her first experience with a huge crowd. She feels the weight of needing to perform well. Instead of harping on dread and jumbling her mind with what if, she returns to a beginner's mind. She prepares herself in her imagination, she re-encounters her moments of pinnacle execution when she presents effectively. As she feels the energy at this moment, she envisions applying them in her new presentations. She realized she needed to connect with her past habits to assist her with growing new ones. She realized that if she distinctively envisioned having another habit, her brain would normally start to rewire to make the physical and mental connection.

John is a business proficient for a manufacturing production network organization that is profoundly partitioned on a significant choice, feeling conflicted and uncertain of his methodology. He knows that his considerations are unfocused and running in various ways while the negative voice inside his head is yelling doubt and fear. He stops it, clears his psyche with a beginner's brain, and sets up useful information-gathering questions that lead to successful improved performance and decision making. Everything that both of these people did was a result of their psychological habits. Despite your field of intrigue, the martial techniques, gives important lessons to anybody confronting difficulties from business, sports, to the fields of art and politics.

## The Weak or Undisciplined Mind

An undisciplined or frail mind is like an "interior foe" or an "internal voice" that authorizes us or entices us to do less. Here are a few instances of a business expert's negative reasoning (your "inward foe"):

When you are tired, this "interior adversary" persuades you that two hours of preparation is sufficient, when you know that four is required.

You make an excuse for your behavior by utilizing your emotions or outside conditions as motivation to be less productive.

You complain about the number of hours you are spending on a presentation or contract.

You plan to practice for the bar exam in two months, but you have neglected to focus on an extraordinary daily study plan.

Rewire your brain by subbing each negative idea with a genuinely charged positive one - and quickly follow up on the positive idea. In the end, with less exertion, your positive idea will turn out to be hard-wired, and you will at that point start to act in an amazing, concentrated way - the consequence of an incredible, centered personality.

## The Three Key Disciplines

There are three mental disciplines - mental toughness, awareness, and focus that are singular aptitudes, however, they work best when they are incorporated. Whatever you do, consult on the phone, negotiate in your office, compose a brief, dissect materials, or react to somebody's feelings -

you will probably approach these abilities at fluctuating degrees.

## Mental Toughness

In a challenge between two similarly skilled business experts or leaders, the mentally stronger one will win. Mental toughness, otherwise called "mental strength," is the capacity to condition your psyche with the goal that you can push on and continue to your most elevated level of execution, regardless of your "feelings" or conditions. Building mental strength is a mind game that instructs you to acknowledge and get ready for life's difficulties over which you have practically no control. This doesn't imply that you are apathetic or cold toward a person or thing. You work to change the quality of your reasoning, which at that point coordinates your speech and actions.

Mental quality determines your ability to bounce back from mistakes, disappointments, and failures. Harping on a negative circumstance digs mental ruts and delivers more mix-ups. You can rewire your thinking by mentally concentrating on how you will positively approach and change a comparative circumstance the next time. Mental strength is additionally your ability to stay cool and hold your feelings under control when you start to feel pressure in any circumstance. When you perceive your very own feelings of pressure, practice intentionally hindering your thoughts and actions, and positively visualizing success. Read the statement below, and dole out a number from 1-10 that best fits how well each statement portrays your response, with 10 being a complete match:

## Bouncing Back from the Past

1. I often worry about making the same error I made in a previous case.
2. If I start my day badly, it is difficult for me to turn my performance around.
3. I always talk about the disappointment of losing my last customer.

## Handling Pressure

1. I easily feel intimidated by and anxious about colleagues who have more experience than I have, and who have more

customers.

2. Keep re-perusing the same information when under time tension.
3. I will become fomented while persuading or convincing somebody or closing a sale or deal depends on how well I convey the information.

## Awareness

Usually, individuals give inadequate regard for what they are doing during a particular circumstance or activity. Awareness or mental sharpness implies that you are completely mindful of your environment condition. You are occupied with every one of the elements of a circumstance or activity. All five of your senses are amazingly elevated and you comprehend what is influencing your mood, responses, and thoughts. A condition of mental sharpness likewise involves utilizing emotional knowledge right then and there in time, understanding the connections among yourself and others, and their connections to one another.

Improve your awareness by stopping all auto-pilot thinking and performing multiple tasks without thought. In case you're in a meeting with a client, for example, do you, without thinking, pick up the telephone and afterward give isolated consideration regarding the two parties? Or when occupied with a telephone discussion, do you consequently grin or nod your head when you recognize an associate in the workplace?

Work on being "in the present moment." Don't divide your attention; be mindful. Block out thoughts of the future or the past, and remain focused solely on what's going on around you. From this elevated state of awareness, you will feel significantly more comfortable, confident, and in control of the present circumstance and your reactions. When you are completely engaged, unremarkable performance blurs away.

### Focus and Effective Thinking

Foolish reasoning is characterized as having uncontrolled, unfocused thoughts. This sort of reasoning happens when you come up short on an unmistakably characterized objective or have not considered all the particular steps you should take to achieve that objective. You are thinking foolishly when you are occupied with a discussion and can't distill its main points, when you delegate tasks to others without having adequately considered the assignments, or when you make a half-hearted commitment.

Then again, focus brings forth viable reasoning. It is purposely sorting out and coordinating your thoughts toward accomplishing a particular outcome. Effective reasoning implies that you focus on an objective and consistently, sanely fill in every one of the means and procedures to arrive at it. Effective reasoning, in any case, doesn't imply that you finish an assignment robotically. Genuinely successful thinking implies that you inventively distinguish and take care of issues.

Effective reasoning envisions procedures and steps. You have prepared and planned to pose the correct questions pertinent to a presentation or conference. You can brainstorm successfully because you realize what the ultimate objective is. When you delegate, you have considered not just what you need a partner to achieve, but how you will monitor that task and give useful input along the way. When you practice these three disciplines habitually, your competitive advantage is "All in your brain." And you're certain to be re-wired to win.

# Chapter 13

# HOW TO REWIRE YOUR BRAIN TO AN ABUNDANCE MENTALITY

When I read "Secrets of the Millionaire Mind" by T. Harv Eker, the way I took a look at being rich as a possibility for me took on a very different significance. At long last, here was somebody putting in plain language what it was that made me unique concerning someone rich and gave me how to do it in an applicable and practical manner.

All through his book, Mr. Eker has what he calls "wealth principles."

The primary principle essentially expresses that our revenue can just develop to the extent that we develop as people.

As indicated by Mr. Eker, how we consider cash begins with our absolute first blueprint. This blueprint is framed by verbal programming, modeling of our conduct on others, and by experiences, we have had during our life.

Without going into the nitty-gritty, let it suffice to say that a significant number of us experience the ill effects of a skewed thought of what it is to be rich and have money. We have been tailored without our conscious knowledge to think with a specific goal in mind. This is what is keeping us poor.

However, our brain can be rewired to think as a rich individual thinks.

Mr. Eker accepts that presentations are an incredible mystery for change and he reliably utilizes assertions all through his book.

The first goes like this with your hand on your heart: "My innermost world makes my external world."

Now touch your head and state: "I have a millionaire mind."

Since I had not been to one of Mr. Eker's Millionaire Mind Intensives yet, I needed to discover a way that would quicken my re-programming endeavors.

I have been in the elective wellbeing field for a long time and have examined a wide range of approaches to recuperate the body and brain.

One exceptionally simple and basic strategy that sparkles in the zone of recuperating the psyche is **EFT**, which represents the <u>Emotional Freedom Technique</u>.

EFT is essentially an emotional version of acupuncture except for needles that aren't fundamental. Rather, you stimulate a well-established peak energy focuses on your body by tapping on them with your fingertips. The procedure is quite easy to remember and is compact so you can do it anywhere.

This next announcement: "I decide to receive better approaches for imagining that help my success and happiness," is an awesome assertion which your psyche accepts, however, your subconscious doesn't.

EFT can accelerate the procedure.

The main affirmation applying the EFT system will be: "Although I have enabled myself to be customized, I deeply and truly acknowledge myself." In EFT, it is essential that you delete the first idea first but you likewise need to show that you don't reprimand it for being how it is.

There are three sections, the sequence, the gamut, and afterward, it closes again with the sequence.

The gamut calibrates the brain, utilizing the brain's innovative side and truly hurries your advancement particularly when the sequence is revamped directly after.

This chapter clarifies that working through any feelings of fear that surfaces concerning ascension is all of the process that encourages you to ascend - by assisting you to rewire your brain.

Let's be honest; you should overcome any feelings of fear you have about rising before you have a possibility of coming to the "tipping point" in the ascension process. (The tipping point is simply where you give your higher self and especially, your internal direction at least as much assurance and consideration as anybody or anything outside of yourself, even the ascension specialists you may pursue strictly, even the diverted messages that originate from Archangel Michael, SaLuSa, or Mathew Ward.)

Several fears can come up as one starts the path of ascension. A portion of these apprehensions emerges from errors spread on the Internet. For instance, a few people are stressed that they may ascend "without wanting to." They need to "remain behind" to deal with friends and family. This, and some other fear, will be worked through before you can make advances into the ascension process.

So, how would you approach discharging your fears? I can ensure that you won't discharge your fears just by saying, "I discharge my fear about rising" or by professing to "let it go" as though you are releasing an balloon up into the climate. You will need to sit down and work through your fear as far as you could tell. You should call upon your higher self and your instinct as well as rationally consider things so that at last, your brain perceives that your fear is ungrounded and feels safe.

By utilizing the reconnecting process (reconnecting with your higher self) and thoroughly considering things, you are making new neural associations that are raising your awareness. You are producing new neural pathways (new extensions to cognizance) in your brain. This implies that you are rewiring your brain and raising your awareness.

No one but you can thoroughly consider things in your very own brain. No one but you can produce new neural associations (that interface your DNA strands together). Cam you currently observe why nobody can actuate your awareness for you and why it's senseless to imagine that you can rise without wanting to? Nobody can interface your DNA strands for you, similarly like nobody can activate your awareness. No one but you can do this for yourself.

At the point when we take a look at the condition of the world, I figure we can concur that something significant must change. Mankind has been modified to follow the lessons of the "high priests" and the "specialists" for a large number of years. Can you truly hope to ascend without figuring out how to have an independent perspective or trust your inward direction? Would a Golden Age even be conceivable with a populace that can't have an independent mind? No way!

I was never terrified of vanishing from the Earth and deserting my friends and family since that situation was never genuine to me, however, I had different feelings of trepidation concerning ascension that I expected to process through. Regardless of the nature of your fear around ascension, processing through them is critical. Working through your feelings of trepidation will help rewire your brain, which encourages you to rise.

# Chapter 14

# FREQUENTLY ASKED QUESTIONS (FAQ)

<u>What does it mean to rewire your brain?</u>

What does it mean to rewire your brain? In one sense, it's trivial: it implies that connections between neurons in your brain are evolving. All that we learn is put away in the brain, and the brain can't store information if it doesn't physically change in some (normally standard) way.

<u>How long does the brain take to rewire?</u>

The brain is continually 'rewiring' itself every time — from hundreds of milliseconds to minutes, to hours, to days, to weeks, etc. This rewiring is commonly called neuroplasticity or plasticity.

<u>Can the brain be rewired?</u>

The development and rewiring of our brain cells is called neuroplasticity. As we learn, our brain truly redesigns itself dependent on our new experiences. Until now, the conventional reasoning was that our brains were designed during childbirth and in this way unchangeable.

<u>How do you rewire your brain for happiness?</u>

Here are a couple of the basic ways science has demonstrated you can rewire your brain to be more joyful:

1. Practice appreciation. Much the same as with an instrument, you can improve your attitude by practicing...
2. Get more rest...
3. Think about your accomplishments…
4. Make a decision…
5. Give a hug or get a massage.

How can I fortify my brain against anxiety?

A balanced diet, ordinary exercise, and a lot of rest are incredible places to begin. Be that as it may, whenever you feel the anxiety starting to crawl up, attempt these three in-the-moment tips to help retrain your anxious brain, and ease anxiety. Taking a few deep breaths is perhaps the least complex way you can help ease anxiety.

Can thoughts change brain chemistry?

It's appeared again and again that simply considering something can make your brain discharge neurotransmitters, chemical messengers that enable it to speak with parts of itself and your sensory system. ... Studies have demonstrated that thoughts alone can improve vision, strength, and fitness.

Can music rewire your brain?

Four Ways Music Can Rewire Your Brain

Listening to music or playing an instrument is what might be compared to a cross-training exercise. The effect of music on memory has been related to complex cognition, perception, and motor function since the milestone "Mozart Effect" study led in 1993.

How can I train my brain to be positive?

Fortunately, you can prepare your brain to turn out to be increasingly positive through these seven strategies.

1. Observe your thoughts. ...
2. Scan for the three daily positives. ...
3. Give someone a shoutout. ...
4. Help others.
5. Surround yourself with positive individuals...
6. Look after your brain and body...
7. Subconscious re-training and inner recovery.

How do you develop neuroplasticity?

Here are five ways to increase and harness the power of neuroplasticity:

1. Get enough quality rest. Your brain needs rest to reset brain connections that are significant for memory and learning.
2. Continue learning and continue moving.
3. Reduce stress.
4. Find a solid purpose for what you intend on learning.
5. Read novels.

# CONCLUSION

The human brain is an advanced development on its own. Just like a computer, your intellectual nerves are modern enough to create the most articulate words, verbalize attractive sounds, and convey the sharpest perspectives on everything. Indeed, there is such a mechanism as rewiring your brain wherein you can incredibly transport smart thoughts pass your desires. This is a procedure called plasticity, and it ought to be given credit since it is what makes you adjust to consistent changes, in innovation, however, in pretty much everything in life.

It's intriguing to realize that the brain is like a relentless machine, trying to work for our reasonable decisions. Our common sense removes us from corrupting circumstances and causes us to settle on sound decisions. Plasticity causes us to loosen up when faced with a strained circumstance. As you can see, the procedure can be both a confidant or treatment, anyway, you might need to take a look at it.

Half-baked thoughts lead to wrong choices.

If your brain isn't rewiring as it regularly should, you could be out of plasticity. This implies you freeze up and stop all capacities when you complete things. This is to your impediment since you would wind up overlooking other methodologies that could assist you with settling on better decisions.

To make sure you are aware, the front parts of your brain work to help you strategize. By not rewiring your brain, these territories incidentally shut down, and you won't be able to think straight. Your idea affects matter because they are conveyed directly to your nerves and mobilized through your activations. Bad trees bear un-scrumptious fruits, which could be compared to half-baked bearing wrong undertakings.

Stimulating the brain is a rewiring plan that is practically identical to the law of vibration. The tremor triggers beats; along these lines, stimulating the brain to work reasonably. Resignation about completing things doesn't invigorate the sensibility in you - or anyone - by any means. Being responsive and active, then again, such as partaking in talks or making a prompt move because of a circumstance, causes you to benefit from the wonders of a total brain rewire.

No competitor in the Olympic Games can gather an award without broad mental and physical training. This abandons saying that a student can't graduate with distinction, nor will an executive get corporate incentives, without having proven flexibility, intelligence, and power in any case. Rewiring your brain encourages you to accomplish all these.

The emergence of digital improved gadgets and advanced correspondence frameworks in this alleged electronic age incites rewiring your brain even more. The mechanisms of the Internet, for example, search engines, emails, and instant messengers demand this. You are stimulating your mind more, contrasted with how it used to be with the more customary strategies for composing snail mail and poring through library books, and so forth. The huge contents of visuals, texts, moving items, and exceptionally mechanical highlights are overhauling your brain with the goal that you accomplish things all the more rapidly. Since everything has now been computerized, you should be smarter and current. All thanks to the brain's plasticity, you likely are.

www.ingramcontent.com/pod-product-compliance
Lightning Source LLC
Chambersburg PA
CBHW020742160726
47993CB00006B/2568